KINGDOM WOMAN

Discover Your Mandate, Mantle, and Ministry

PATRICIA GARLAND

KINGDOM WOMAN by Patricia Garland
PO Box 9051
Waukegan, IL 60085

This book or parts thereof may not be reproduced in any form, stored in a retrieval system, or transmitted in any form by any means—electronic, mechanical, photocopy, recording, or otherwise—without prior written permission of the publisher, except as provided by United States of America copyright law.

Unless otherwise noted, all Scripture quotations are from the King James Version of the Bible.

Scripture quotations marked AMP are from the Amplified Bible. Copyright © 1954, 1958, 1962, 1964, 1965, 1987 by The Lockman Foundation. Used by permission.

Scripture quotations marked ESV are from the Holy Bible, English Standard Version. Copyright © 2001 by Crossway Bibles, a division of Good News Publishers. Used by permission.

Scripture quotations marked NIV are taken from the Holy Bible, New International Version®, NIV®. Copyright © 1973, 1978, 1984, 2011 by Biblica, Inc.™ Used by permission of Zondervan. All rights reserved worldwide. www.zondervan.com The "NIV" and "New International Version" are trademarks registered in the United States Patent and Trademark Office by Biblica, Inc.

Scripture quotations marked NKJV are from the New King James Version of the Bible. Copyright © 1979, 1980, 1982 by Thomas Nelson, Inc., publishers. Used by permission.

Scripture quotations marked THE MESSAGE are from The Message: The Bible in Contemporary English, copyright © 1993, 1994, 1995, 1996, 2000, 2001, 2002. Used by permission of NavPress Publishing Group.

Scripture quotations marked NLT are from the Holy Bible, New Living Translation, copyright © 1996, 2004, 2015 by Tyndale House Foundation. Used by permission of Tyndale House Publishers, Inc., Carol Stream, IL 60188. All rights reserved.

Scripture quotations marked TLB are from The Living Bible. Copyright © 1971. Used by permission of Tyndale House Publishers, Inc., Wheaton, IL 60189. All rights reserved.

Copyright © 2019 by Patricia Garland
All rights reserved

Visit the author's website at www.patriciaagarland.com.
International Standard Book Number: 978-1-73387-302-4
E-book ISBN: 978-1-73387-303-1

While the author has made every effort to provide accurate internet addresses at the time of publication, neither the publisher nor the author assumes any responsibility for errors or for changes that occur after publication. Further, the publisher does not have any control over and does not assume any responsibility for author or third-party websites or their content.

19 20 21 22 23 — 987654321
Printed in the United States of America

To my Lord and Savior Jesus Christ, my King, I love You and worship You.

To my mother, Dorothy: God gave you so many gifts and talents. I thank you for imparting so much into my life. Thanks for being a great mother. You had a desire to preach the gospel and build the Lord a house. This book is especially for you, Mom. I'm sure you are pleased that I am living out your dream.

To my father, Albert: I was honored to lead you to the Lord. There was nothing more exciting than seeing you going to church and to see you serving with me in ministry. I miss hearing you cheer me on. I'm sure you are cheering from heaven.

To my husband, my hero and honey, Pastor Bobby: You have taught me so much about life. You are a great husband, father, and man of God. Many men do not support their wives in the vision God has given them. Thank you for supporting me in ministry. I appreciate you, I honor you, and I love you.

To my adult children, Tikwan, Tikina, Tikori, and Tikwhayla: I know it was not always easy with my being in ministry and having to share me with so many others. I will always cherish the times we spent in the morning praying and memorizing scriptures before you went to school. I'm thankful today that I now have the privilege to receive prayers and scriptures from you. What a blessing from the Lord. I love you all dearly.

To my grandchildren, Keilonn, Kyla, Hannah, Kingston, Thiland, and Kori Jr.; my sisters, Dorothy and Lorraine; and my brothers, John, Harvey, James, Larry, and Vincent: I love you.

To my pastors, Apostle John and Prophetess Wanda Eckhardt: Thank you for imparting the apostolic mantle into my life. I am forever grateful.

To all my family, friends, and spiritual children: Thank you all for your love, support, encouragement, and most of all believing in me. You all have inspired me to be the woman of God I am today. I love you all.

CONTENTS

Foreword by John Eckhardt ix
Introduction: Becoming a Kingdom Woman xi

PART 1: THE MANDATE

Chapter 1: Who Is the Kingdom Woman? 1
Chapter 2: The Character of the Kingdom Woman 9
Chapter 3: The Kingdom Woman on a Mission 41
Chapter 4: The Kingdom Woman—Tested and Proven, Delivered and Set Free 57

PART 2: THE MANTLE

Chapter 5: Anointed and Called 91
Chapter 6: A Woman of Prayer 97
Chapter 7: Authority, Power, and Demonstration 107

PART 3: THE MINISTRY

Chapter 8: What Does the Bible Say About Women in Ministry and Leadership? 121
Chapter 9: The Kingdom Woman and Divine Alliances 137
Chapter 10: The Kingdom Woman Preparing for Fivefold Ministry 149
Chapter 11: The Kingdom Woman Serving in Fivefold Ministry 167

Chapter 12:	The Kingdom Woman: a Legacy of Influence	179
Epilogue:	A Prophetic Word to the Kingdom Woman: Arise and Shine!	193
Appendix:	Womanology	199
Notes		205

FOREWORD

I AM HONORED TO write the foreword for Patricia Garland's new book, *Kingdom Woman*. Patricia and her husband, Bobby, have faithfully served at the church I lead, Crusaders Church in Chicago. Over the years I have seen God perfect in her the characteristics of a kingdom woman.

As an overseer in the body of Christ, it has always been in my heart to raise up and promote strong and godly women. For years, I have been preaching, writing books, and leading conferences centered on the power of a virtuous woman—a woman of valor, might, wealth, and strong moral character. The Bible uses the Hebrew word *chayil* to describe her; Patricia Garland is calling out to her as "kingdom woman."

This message is important in this season. Women need to be confident in pursuing the call of God on their lives. Women also need to be empowered and promoted in the areas of their gifting. The body of Christ should be leading in this area. We need to empower women to be all God has called them to be—and that extends beyond being the great mothers and wives many of them are. In addition to that, we need more women preachers, ministers, prophets, teachers, evangelists, prophets, and apostles. We need to encourage women who serve in the marketplace as entrepreneurs, CEOs, administrators, civil servants, philanthropists, and humanitarians. We need kingdom women in every sphere of culture—women who lead and serve with the power and might of God.

I believe we will see the kingdom of God increase exponentially when we allow women to return to their rightful place as the corulers God created them to be.

The thing that I appreciate about this book is that, in it, Patricia is honest and transparent about her own journey to becoming a kingdom woman. A wife, mother, and ministry leader herself, she also connects the stories of leading women in the Bible such as Deborah, Esther, Huldah, Mary, Naomi, Pheobe, Lydia, Junia, and more to their modern counterparts still being birthed today. She also includes an historical tribute to women of faith who were martyrs, champions of the faith, ministers, reformers, denominational leaders, and workers of miracles and the supernatural.

Her careful study and passion to see women walk in the power of God is felt on every page. You will be blessed as you read this book.

If you are coming to this book as a woman seeking the Lord for your destiny and purpose, you will be led closer to it. If you lead a woman's ministry or mentor women, you will find this book to be an essential resource to aid your efforts. If you are a man, you will gain a godly view of kingdom women and learn new ways to encourage, accept, and appreciate the strength who they are and their value in life and ministry. I believe that all who read this book will be blessed by it and motivated to take up its charge.

—JOHN ECKHARDT
BEST-SELLING AUTHOR, *PRAYERS THAT ROUT DEMONS*
AND *WOMEN'S DAILY DECLARATIONS*
FOR SPIRITUAL WARFARE
OVERSEER, CRUSADERS CHURCH OF CHICAGO

Introduction

BECOMING A KINGDOM WOMAN

THE LORD SAYS, "I am raising up trendsetters—those who will not follow the old trend of traditions but those who will set the tone. They will carry the torch of My scepter. New trendsetters and trailblazers will arise with fire in their eyes, fire in their mouths, and fire in their hands to arise to set the standard of holiness and righteousness."

The Lord says, "I'm raising up new trendsetters who will start movements of miracles and manifestations of My glory. Trendsetters who are authentic. Trendsetters who are unique. Trendsetters who will lead the way to the light in the midst of darkness. Trendsetters who will cry aloud and lift up their voices like trumpets. Trendsetters who are initiators and innovators. Trendsetters who will not be afraid to tread upon serpents and scorpions. Trendsetters who will roar like lions. Trendsetters who will soar like eagles."

Woman of the kingdom, God is raising up women who are trendsetters like you. Their style and trend will not be of the flesh, but their spirit, style, and trend will be of the kingdom. Their trend will be majestic. Their style and trend will be glorious. They will be kingdom women who have been created in the image and likeness of God. They will arise and be fruitful. They will be women like you who will multiply, replenish the earth, and subdue it. These women will have dominion.

God is raising up women who have been in darkness. He is restoring brightness to them. These are women who have been hidden. No one knows who they are, but like you, they will be renowned. They will carry God's majesty. Like you, the unspoken manifestation of God's glory shall be seen upon them, and they will arise and rejoice.

Woman of God, you have been created for His glory. You are a glory carrier in the earth. You are designed to walk in power, authority, and dominion.

God is calling you, kingdom woman. Where are you, Deborah, Esther, Jael, and Ruth—women who are prepared to make a difference in our generation?

Kingdom woman, your time has come and your light is rising. You are a leader like Deborah, an intercessor like Esther, a prophet like Huldah, a godly mother like Mary, a godly grandmother like Naomi, an evangelist like the Samaritan woman at the well, a woman with a servant heart like Phoebe, or a Christian businesswoman like Lydia.

Although the things God has laid aside for you will have similar qualities to what these women had, God has designed a life and ministry just for you. Whatever position you are in now—whether you are functioning in your calling, wondering how to get started, feeling stuck in the traditions of men, or if you are running in the opposite direction like Jonah—God wants to speak to you and move you forward.

Woman of God, I wrote this book for you. *Kingdom Woman* is not about a woman's liberation movement or usurping man's authority. This book is a decree set forth to develop a kingdom mentality for both men and women, to establish God's principles that His Kingdom is first and foremost. "But seek ye first the kingdom of God, and His righteousness; and all these things shall be added unto you" (Matt. 6:33). This book has been designed to bring clarity to believers about the life of a kingdom woman.

This is a decree set forth to restore balance in the body of Christ.

Simply put, this book is designed to encourage you, and to give you biblical insight that will help you become a kingdom woman and discover God's unique plan for your life—your ministry, family, and business life. God's purpose from the beginning, when He formed woman from man's side, was to be a helpmeet. Men and women, and husbands and wives can benefit from the gifts God has given to each of them. Like iron that sharpens iron to release synergy to strengthen and advance the kingdom, so is the balance of men and women coming together in unity. It is important for us to know that God has called women as well as men to do great things in the kingdom.

This book will encourage you not to walk in fear, but to walk in faith to discover the treasure God has put inside of you. I will share revelations God has given me about His nature and character toward women. I will share what God has shown me about the place women have in His kingdom and their responsibilities. I will share with you strategies for how to discern the nature of your unique calling, how to overcome obstacles, and how to walk in your calling. Throughout the Bible, those who were chosen had to overcome many challenges. I will teach you what the Lord showed me about how to stand against all odds, endure, and become strong in the Lord. You will discover your mandate, mantle, and ministry and become the kingdom woman God has designed you to be.

I pray that this teaching will encourage, equip, and empower you to become extraordinary. I pray that you will get the resources you need to step forward into the full calling of God to be a kingdom woman. I pray that whether you are a prophet, apostle, pastor, teacher, evangelist, wife, mother, professional, or student, you will see yourself reflected in these pages and you will gain the boldness and courage to step out from being common to become uncommon, unusual, and unique—to become the trendsetter that God has designed you to be. Enjoy the journey of the making of a kingdom woman.

PART ONE
THE MANDATE

Chapter 1

WHO IS THE KINGDOM WOMAN?

And when he was demanded of the Pharisees, when the kingdom of God should come, he answered them and said, The kingdom of God cometh not with observation: Neither shall they say, Lo here! or lo there! for, behold, the kingdom of God is within you.
—LUKE 17:20–21

SIMPLY PUT, THE kingdom woman is a woman who is a citizen of the kingdom of God. The kingdom is a spiritual kingdom—it is invisible to the natural eye—and its King is the God of Abraham, Isaac, and Jacob. The kingdom woman serves and loves this King with all her heart, soul, and mind. But there's more to this that I would like to reveal.

Let's look at the verse above. What did Jesus mean when He said, "The kingdom of God cometh not with observation"? The Greek word *parateresis* is used here for the English word *observation*. It means "hostile watching."[1] The Pharisees were watching for the coming of the kingdom with hostility, but Jesus wanted them to understand that the kingdom was not coming in the way they had anticipated. He went on to explain that the kingdom of God is "within you." The Greek word for "within" is *entos*, which means "in the midst of you."[2] This is saying that the King of the kingdom of heaven, who is the earthly aspect of the universal kingdom of God, is in the midst of you now, but you will not recognize Him because the kingdom of which Jesus spoke is spiritual, not earthly.

According to Webster's Dictionary, *kingdom* is "a politically organized community or major territorial unit having a monarchical form of government headed by a king or queen."[3] When referring to God, *kingdom* means "the eternal kingship of God" and "the realm in which God's will is fulfilled."[4] In the original Greek writing of the New Testament, the word for "kingdom" is *basileia*, which means "kingship, sovereignty, authority, and rule, especially of God, both in the world and in the hearts of men."[5] A kingdom always requires a monarch or a head of state, and the kingdom of God has King Jesus.

The word *kingdom* is constantly used throughout the Bible in connection with the rule of Christ in the hearts of believers. The kingdom, which is of heavenly or divine origin and nature, is the rule in power. That same power has been given to us as believers. Jesus said, "I give unto you power to tread on serpents and scorpions, and over all the powers of the enemy: and nothing shall by any means hurt you" (Luke 10:19).

When we speak of being women of the kingdom, we are not just speaking about being everyday, average believers. We are talking about kingdom women—uncommon and unusual women who have been given authority, power, and influence to shift lives, cities, and governments for the kingdom of God. A kingdom woman has power to impact, empower and influence the lives of others. This means that there is also a difference between the church and the kingdom. The church is a place where people come together to have organizational meetings and do things according to customs and traditions. The *kingdom of God* is the place people of every nation who believe in Him gather together into one society, dedicated and intimately united with God and made partakers of eternal salvation. This kingdom has now begun and is actually present inasmuch as its foundations have already been laid by Christ.

Woman of God, we are kingdom citizens and kingdom ambassadors sent to represent the King of kings. (See Psalm 24:8–10.) People who are stuck in church mentalities do not fully understand kingdom principles and patterns and most likely may not receive all that the kingdom of God has to offer. They only understand what has been passed down through the tradition and religion of the church.

Jesus says, "Behold, the kingdom of God is within you." It's within the believer, which means His kingship is within you. His authority is within you. His power is within you to rule and reign from His kingdom. But some believers allow their kingdom power and authority to lie dormant instead of activating that authority that is within them.

> These twelve Jesus sent forth, and commanded them, saying, Go not into the way of the Gentiles, and into any city of Samaritans enter ye not: But go rather to the lost sheep of the house of Israel. And as ye go, preach, saying, the kingdom of heaven is

> at hand. Heal the sick, cleanse the lepers, raise the dead, cast out devils: freely ye have received, freely give.
>
> —MATTHEW 10:5–8

There are many believers who say they are in the kingdom, but they don't believe in healing the sick, cleansing the lepers, raising the dead, and casting out devils. A true sign that you are a part of God's kingdom is that you believe in flowing in the supernatural. The Bible says, "And these signs shall follow them that believe; In my name shall they cast out devils; they shall speak with new tongues; They shall take up serpents; and if they drink any deadly thing, it shall not hurt them; they shall lay hands on the sick, and they shall recover" (Mark 16:17–18).

Take It Back

If the enemy has blinded you or stolen godly principles from you, it is up to you to take it back. God is raising up a mighty army of women to advance His kingdom: you can be a light that will shine in the midst of the kingdom of darkness. Matthew 11:12 says, "From the days of John the Baptist until now the kingdom of heaven suffereth violence, and the violent take it by force."

Kingdom women are not afraid to take back what rightfully belongs to them. For these are the days that women will rise up and take back their families, finances, states, cities, communities, schools, and nations for the kingdom of God through prayer and intercession. Kingdom women are rising up to reclaim the seven mountains, which are the mountain of arts, mountain of business, mountain of education, mountain of family, mountain of government, mountain of media, and the mountain of religion.

The kingdom of God is actively moving and gaining momentum, and God's kingdom women take on its attributes. "For the kingdom is the LORD's," Psalm 22:28 says, "and he is the governor among the nations." Romans 14:17 says, "For the kingdom of God is not meat and drink; but righteousness, and peace, and joy in the Holy Ghost." A kingdom woman walks in righteousness, peace, and joy in serving her King. She is set apart and does not look like the world, she does not act like the world, she does not talk like the world, and she does not dress like the world. For John 18:36 says, "My kingdom is not of this world." The Bible speaks of two kingdoms— the kingdom of light and the kingdom of darkness. The kingdom woman is of the kingdom of light, an ambassador for righteousness. The light of Jesus shines and is radiant upon her countenance. In the midst of the kingdom of darkness, she shines and stands out with brightness and boldness.

How Do I Become a Kingdom Woman?

Up to this point, we've talked about the big picture— the kingdom of God, in which the heart of the kingdom woman resides, and how the kingdom is within her. There is so much power, victory, and freedom to be experienced by all who are of this kingdom. But you may have been reading along and realized that you have been living outside the kingdom looking in. Maybe you are reading this and wondering how you too can feel the power of God and how you can experience becoming a kingdom woman. The Bible says, "It is in Him that we live and move and have our being (Acts 17:28). In other words, without God we can do nothing. We must yield to God to allow Him to live and move and have the activity of our being. This is why I want to stop here and extend an invitation for you to become part of the kingdom of God. You may have only experienced being apart of church, which we spoke about earlier, but I think this is an important pause just before we get into the characteristics of the kingdom woman and all that God has in store for her. I want to offer you an opportunity to join this exclusive group and take part in all of its benefits.

Jesus took a similar pause from His everyday ministry to sit and talk with someone who wanted to know how to join the kingdom of God. This story is found in the book of John, chapter 3. Jesus took time out to meet with a Pharisee named Nicodemus. Let's look at what Jesus revealed to him about becoming a citizen of the kingdom. The scripture reads:

> There was a man of the Pharisees, named Nicodemus, a ruler of the Jews:
> The same came to Jesus by night, and said unto him, Rabbi, we know that thou art a teacher come from God: for no man can do these miracles that thou doest, except God be with him.
> Jesus answered and said unto him, Verily, verily, I say unto thee, Except a man be born again, he cannot see the kingdom of God.
> Nicodemus saith unto him, How can a man be born when he is old? can he enter the second time into his mother's womb, and be born?
> Jesus answered, Verily, verily, I say unto thee, Except a man be born of water and of the Spirit,

he cannot enter into the kingdom of God. That which is born of the flesh is flesh; and that which is born of the Spirit is spirit. Marvel not that I said unto thee, Ye must be born again.

—JOHN 3:1–7

Just like each of us was born into this world, born into a particular family, we too must be born into the kingdom of God, a spiritual kingdom. Some of us may have been born into poor families and have wished we were born into rich families. When we are born into God's kingdom—God's family, we receive kingdom benefits of His wealth and riches. Psalm 112:3 says, "Wealth and riches shall be in his house: and his righteousness endureth forever."

In order to be born into God's spiritual kingdom family, you have to experience a spiritual birth. There are some who think they can be born again by the flesh, like Nicodemus thought. But you cannot be born into the kingdom of God by natural birth. It must be spiritual. Flesh gives birth to flesh, but Spirit gives birth to Spirit. If you want to see the kingdom, Jesus said you must be born again. And unless you are born of water and the Spirit, you cannot enter the kingdom of God. Becoming a kingdom woman takes more than going to church and getting the right hand of fellowship. You must be born into the kingdom. You must be born of the Spirit.

If you would like to take your first real step toward becoming a kingdom woman, I invite you to make this declaration with me:

Father, it is my heart's desire to experience a new birth to receive kingdom benefits. Your

> Word declares in Luke 12:32, "Fear not, little flock, for it is your Father's good pleasure to give you the kingdom" (ESV). I decree and declare that I will not be afraid to walk in all that you have ordained for me as a kingdom woman. In Jesus's name. Amen.

Now you have received your new birth as a kingdom woman. With your new identity as a kingdom woman, you join a bold and mighty army of women.

In the next chapter, you will learn what this kingdom woman is like, what her characteristics are, and what sets her apart.

Chapter 2

THE CHARACTER OF THE KINGDOM WOMAN

For God so loved the world, that he gave his only begotten Son, that whosoever believeth in him should not perish, but have everlasting life.
—JOHN 3:16

God's kingdom is governed by God's love, and one of the first character traits a kingdom woman must exhibit is the love of God. Some women have a difficult time loving themselves and therefore struggle to demonstrate love to other women. Kingdom woman, you must embrace God's love for you so that you can embrace other women in love. Although you have read the verse printed above and others like it many times, you may still struggle with feelings that God doesn't love you.

Maybe you grew up in a family where your father did not affirm his love to you. Maybe you grew up in a family where love was not demonstrated and you went through life feeling rejected, unwanted, and unloved. I grew up without hearing my daddy say, "I love you." He also grew up without his daddy telling him, "I love you."

You can break that bloodline curse of rejection and feeling unloved. Settle it in your heart that not only did God so loved the world, but more specifically and uniquely, God so loved you that He gave His only begotten Son to die on a cross for your sins. It doesn't matter what kind of background you come from or what you have done. God did this for you because He loves you and wanted nothing to keep you from being with Him. Sin separates us from God. But through Jesus's sacrifice, a way was made for you to become one with God.

God loves you, and when you know you are loved by God, you are compelled to love Him enough to obey Him. The Bible says, "If you love Me, keep My commandments" (John 14:15, NKJV). Many of us struggle to obey the call of God on our lives because we have not fully developed a genuine love for God. He is calling out to us, "If you love Me, you will keep My command, My call, and My destiny for your life."

God will circumcise your heart so that you will love the Lord (Deut. 30:6). The word *circumcise* that appears in this Old Testament verse means that "God will *change* your heart...so that you will love him" (NLT, emphasis added). He does this by drawing you by His lovingkindness. He says through the prophet Jeremiah, "Yea, I have loved thee with an everlasting love: therefore with lovingkindness have I drawn thee" (Jer. 31:3). When you understand God's love and faithfulness toward you and when you have learned to love God, you will begin to see yourself and others through the loving eyes of God. You will love your neighbors as you love yourself (Matt.

22:39). You will be empowered to love the unlovable—sinners, backsliders, and those who are hurting, abused, oppressed, and outcast. Love covers a multitude of sins (1 Pet. 4:8).

I believe that love is a very important issue many have misinterpreted. There are different languages of love. Here are four of them listed with their Greek names and English meaning:

- *Agape*—unconditional love
- *Philia*—brotherly love, as shown between siblings and close friends
- *Eros*—intimate love between husband and wife
- *Storge*—love between parents and children and other members of a family

Jesus, who is our greatest example of love, demonstrated these types of love for all mankind. Jesus loves us unconditionally. There is nothing we can do that will stop the Lord from loving us.

God has demonstrated such amazing love toward us even when we were sinning and didn't deserve His love (Rom. 5:8). How many of us would be willing to give our only son? Praise God that He is not asking us to give our son or daughter. He has already given the ultimate sacrifice so that we may have life and life more abundantly (John 10:10). Now He is asking that we return that love to Him, our family, friends, neighbors, and ourselves.

God Chastens Those He Loves

Something that every kingdom woman should expect in her love relationship with God is to be chastened, corrected, disciplined, trained, and fine-tuned to carry out the call on our lives to completion. His correction comes as a result of His great love for us. Hebrews 12:6 says, "For whom the Lord loveth he chasteneth, and scourgeth every son whom he receiveth." We should welcome the refinement of the Lord.

The earlier years of my marriage were some of the darkest days of my life. I did not know if I would ever see light. One day I was on my knees crying out to God, saying, "Lord, what have I ever done so bad to receive this much heartache and pain in my life?" I thought maybe God did not love me. I thought God was angry at me. But He assured me that He was not angry with me, that He had an assignment for me. The Lord answered me, very profoundly, saying, "Pat, what you are going through is not for you. It is for someone else."

I did not understand what the Lord was saying at the time, but years later I came to understand that God's lessons in love were to help me demonstrate unconditional love to my husband who came from a broken, dysfunctional family. It was for the sake of my husband that I was being challenged in my love walk. I was also being chastened by the Lord. He was imparting His unconditional love for my husband through my character. There were times I felt like giving up, but the Lord kept reminding me that what I was going through was not for me, but for someone else. You see, it's easy to love people who love you, but can you love people who don't love you back? My husband was not in a right state of mind to love me the God kind of way because he simply didn't know how to love himself, therefore, he couldn't love me back.

Through my process of praying and fasting for my marriage, God was teaching me how to love the unlovable, and to love my husband unconditionally. By teaching me this within my marriage, the Lord was also preparing me for ministry, although I didn't know the Lord was preparing me for ministry until years later. He had a plan for me to minister to other hurting women and men. It was not easy. Today I can honestly say that I see how God brought salvation, healing, deliverance, and restoration to my marriage and to many other marriages by empowering me through His love to help women and men find their way to their own restoration, healing, and deliverance. I have been able to see so many set free because of the lessons God taught me. Now I can say that it was worth every tear and every pain. Salvation, deliverance, and redemption were the end results in my husband's life after God teaching me to walk in God's unconditional love. Throughout my book, I will give you a glimpse of more testimonies of things I had to learn in my marriage to become an overcoming kingdom woman. We overcame him by him by the blood of the Lamb and the words of our testimony (Rev. 12:11).

The Bible says, "Greater love hath no man than this, that a man lay down his life for his friends" (John 15:13). This is exactly what God led me to do in my marriage. My husband is my friend, and it took dying to myself every day to reflect Christ's love in a way that he would understand it.

I believe God wants to teach you about His

unconditional love. In times when you feel the chastening of the Lord, don't run from Him. Run to Him. In doing so, you will develop the love with which God has marked His kingdom woman.

There are so many gifted, talented, and anointed people who can pray, preach, and prophesy, but where are the people who walk in the love of God? The Bible says that God's people will be known by their love (John 13:35) not by their gifts and anointing. I'm sad to say it, but some may even put on façades and pretend to love God's people. The world may not know the Greek and Hebrew words for the different types of love, but they know the language of real, genuine, and authentic love when they see it. And when they don't see it from people who claim to be part of the family of God, they will know something is not right.

THE LOVE TEST

> Though I speak with the tongues of men and of angels, and have not charity, I am become as sounding brass, or a tinkling cymbal. And though I have the gift of prophecy, and understand all mysteries, and all knowledge; and though I have all faith, so that I could remove mountains, and have not charity, I am nothing. And though I bestow all my goods to feed the poor, and though I give my body to be burned, and have not charity, it profiteth me nothing.
>
> Charity suffereth long, and is kind; charity envieth not; charity vaunteth not itself, is not puffed up, doth not behave itself unseemly, seeketh not her own, is not easily provoked, thinketh no evil; rejoiceth not in iniquity, but rejoiceth in

the truth; beareth all things, believeth all things, hopeth all things, endureth all things.
—1 Corinthians 13:1–7

In school you were given final examinations, and you had to pass them before you could go to the next grade. I believe in order for God to trust you with His kingdom and the lives of His people you must pass the test of love.

Kingdom women are filled with the genuine love of God. They suffer long. They do not give up easily. Kingdom women are kind. Kingdom women are not envious. Kingdom women are not jealous or puffed up in pride. Kingdom women do not behave unseemly or seek their own way. Kingdom women are not easily provoked and think no evil. Kingdom women do not rejoice in iniquity, but they rejoice in truth. Kingdom women bear all things, believe all things, hope all things, and endure all things. Kingdom women do not just flow in the gifts of the Spirit, professional skills, or natural talents, but they also walk in character and integrity driven by the love of God. This love compels kingdom women to demonstrate the love of the Lord by embracing, encouraging, and empowering other women, their brothers in Christ, and the hurting, lost, and broken. If you are going to be a kingdom woman, you must develop kindness as an ambassador of the kingdom of love.

The Unfailing Loyalty of Love

I'll say this again, love your neighbor as you love yourself. Don't be a woman who flows in the gifts but does not flow in God's love. I have seen too many people get hurt and leave the church because some people stand in the pulpit and say how much they love God but do not demonstrate the love of God to others. The Bible says, "If a man say, I love God, and hateth his brother, he is a liar: for he that loveth not his brother whom he hath seen, how can he love God whom he hath not seen?" (1 John 4:20). There is no love like God's love. May we welcome the opportunities God provides to grow and develop in His love.

A Woman of War

> Finally, my brethren, be strong in the Lord, and in the power of his might. Put on the whole armour of God, that ye may be able to stand against the wiles of the devil.
> —Ephesians 6:10–11

You've heard it said that "All is fair in love and war," but what a kingdom woman goes to war for is different than what is meant by this saying. It would seem that war is the opposite of love, but they are closely related in the realm of the kingdom. Let me explain.

As a kingdom woman, you don't have an option about your position in the kingdom of God. You automatically become drafted into God's spiritual army. You are in a spiritual war, not against flesh and blood but against principalities, powers, rulers of darkness, and spiritual wickedness in high places (Eph. 6:12). The spiritual enemy of God is your spiritual enemy as well. His name is Satan, and he will not stand by and watch you pursue your purpose. He hates everything that God loves and favors, therefore, he will try to stop you, but you must take your purpose by force.

There are so many believers and nonbelievers who struggle with spirits that are not of God, such as the spirits of fear, rejection, hurt, disappointment, bitterness, unforgiveness, anger, pride, rebellion, witchcraft, lust, perversion, lying, deception, abuse, adultery, religious spirits, generational curses, depression, and sickness and diseases, such as cancer, diabetes, high blood pressure, stroke, and more.

The list of the ways the enemy attacks is almost endless, but there are still some people who don't believe they can be attacked by demonic spirits. Many still don't believe that deliverance is for today, but they cannot deny that they have struggled with at least one or more of the spirits I listed above.

How the Lord Taught My Hands to War (Psalm 144:1)

Though I will talk more about the spirit of fear and how to overcome it in a later chapter, I do want to share a couple of my own encounters with this spirit as it relates to my experience of growing in the ability to win battles against the enemy. Through my bouts with fear, I too became a woman of war.

Fear is a spirit that tormented and paralyzed me most of my life. Like me at the time, many of you may not be walking in your calling because of fear, but you must rise up and decree, "God has not given me the spirit of fear but of power, love, and a sound mind" (2 Tim. 1:7). If you are going to help set the captive free you first must learn how to use your weapons of spiritual warfare (2 Cor. 10:4) to free yourself from strongholds that have held you in bondage.

The devil plants seeds of fear in us early in our childhood, hoping that fear will cause us to be afraid to answer the call. I remember when I was a little girl how every time it would rain, an old man with a white beard would appear in our window with chains. Not only did I see him but my two sisters, with whom I shared a bed, saw him too. It frightened us so badly that we would pull the covers over our heads until he went away. Whether you believe it or not, it was a ghost that tormented my sisters and me for years. We often stayed up late not wanting to go to sleep, because we were afraid that we would see the man who would appear in the window. We later learned that a man had died in that house and came back as a ghost. For years, I thought fear was just a necessary part of my life, until I begin to discover through God's Word that He had not given me "the spirit of fear; but power, and of love, and of a sound mind" (2 Tim. 1:7).

To understand what is at work when it comes to spiritual warfare, you must understand that there are two kingdoms—the kingdom of darkness and the kingdom of light. You must know the forces of darkness that seek to destroy you and your family. God taught me this years ago while I was in spiritual warfare and deliverance training. I would have several strange, demonic dreams. I will not share the details of what I saw, but the dreams were very frightening and concerned the kingdom of darkness. In one dream, God had taken me to what appeared to be a dungeon where witches and warlocks were sacrificing children and animals and drinking their blood. The Lord said to me, "Look at what they are doing." The witches and warlocks would receive higher ranking and more power through Satan when they killed animals and kidnapped children to use as sacrifices. Can you image how frightened I was after waking up in a cold sweats and having demonic dreams about the kingdom of darkness? Satan is strategic and wants to invoke fear, but God has not given us a spirit of fear but of power, love, and a sound mind.

WOMEN OF COURAGE AND BOLDNESS

Kingdom women are bold and courageous. Filled with the Spirit of God, they will take out the spiritual enemies of God by any means necessary. Using her influence, a kingdom woman leads other saints in the charge, as she proclaims, "Give me my mountain!" Two such kingdom women in the Old Testament used their courage and boldness to take over mountains of influence during their time. The first one is Jael.

Jael

"Decisive and courageous, [Jael]...seized the opportunity to slay an enemy of God's people." Her name means "a wild or mountain goat."[1] Judges 4:17–24 tells the story of her bravery:

> Howbeit Sisera fled away on his feet to the tent of Jael the wife of Heber the Kenite: for there was peace between Jabin the king of Hazor and the house of Heber the Kenite. And Jael went out to meet Sisera, and said unto him, turn in, my lord, turn in to me; fear not. And when he had turned in unto her into the tent, she covered him with a mantle.
>
> And he said unto her, give me I pray thee, a little water to drink; for I am thirsty. And she opened a bottle of milk, and gave him a cup of milk, and covered him. Again he said unto her, Stand in the door of the tent, and it shall be, when any man

doth come and enquire of thee, and say, Is there any man here that thou shall say, No.

Then Jael Heber's wife took a nail of the tent, and took an hammer in her hand, and went softly unto him, and hit the nail into his temples, and fastened it into the ground; for he was fast asleep and weary. So he died.

By the will of God, Jael helped saved Israel from long bondage to bitter enemies. This spared the daughters of Israel from horrible tragedies, and the men from destruction at the hands of Sisera.

Kingdom woman, you don't ask the devil permission to save God's people from bondage. You take a nail of the tent and a hammer in your hand, and you drive the nail into the devil's temples, nailing his head to the ground. Remember the devil doesn't fight fair. He comes to steal, kill, and destroy (John 10:10). As you remain in the presence of God, He will give you spiritual strategies to beat the devil at his game.

Now let's turn our attention to another kingdom woman who used her position of influence to boldly demand freedom for her people—Queen Esther.

Esther

It cost Esther her values, beliefs, faith, and dignity to leave her family. It took courage to leave everything she had ever known to be put in a very challenging situation. She had to hide her true identity and be entered into a beauty contest. Perhaps she suffered the same kind of humiliation ex-queen Vashti had to endure, being forced to expose herself in front of the king's friends and to do other inappropriate sexual things—even as a young girl.

Some of you may have been put in humiliating or sexually inappropriate situations growing up.

Kingdom woman, ask yourself the question, What are you willing to leave or let go of in order to fulfill your purpose and destiny? Are you ready for your beliefs, faith, or dignity to be challenged? You may have to leave your traditional church where they do not believe in women pastors or women apostles. You may have to leave your grandmother's church. You may be humiliated, but that may be the cost of courage for a kingdom woman.

At first Esther was reluctant to go to the king on behalf of her people because entering the king's presence without being called could mean death. But Mordecai, who was her older cousin and guardian, encouraged her with a question: "Who knoweth whether thou art come to the kingdom for such a time as this?" (Esther 4:14).

Like Esther, you have been given a mandate for such a time as this—a mandate to show forth your royal position in the kingdom of God. I also implore you to learn this: Esther—having the great attributes of courage and being full of faith—understood the importance of obedience and submission to God and His plan.

> Now when every maid's turn was come to go in to king Ahasuerus, after that she had been twelve months, according to the manner of the women, (for so were the days of their purifications accomplished, to wit, six months with oil of myrrh, and six months with sweet odours, and with other things for the purifying of the women).
> —Esther 2:12

It was not just Esther's beauty that gave her favor with the king when she needed it most; it was also her humility. Although the enemy released a plan of annihilation and total destruction of God's people, God raised up Esther. Through her obedience she became queen and brought deliverance to her family and all of God's people.

WOMAN OF DOMINION

> And God blessed them, and God said unto them, be fruitful, and multiply, and replenish the earth, and subdue it: and have dominion over the fish of the sea, and over the fowl of the air, and over every living thing that moveth upon the earth.
> —GENESIS 1:28

At the time that God made man and woman, He gave them both dominion over the whole earth and everything in it. There is no blind side. God gave equal authority to man and woman while they were living in a sinless state. What happened? In the next few chapters of Genesis, we discover that sin came into the heart of Adam and Eve. They both were given instructions which they both failed to follow. "The result was a temporary curse placed upon both man and woman that would affect the whole earth."[2]

I often say that if a husband and wife can raise a family together, what's wrong with them raising a village, a community, a church and ministry, or a business together? Not many people embrace the concept of a husband and wife team as co-pastors. They will embrace the husband only as the pastor and the wife as an evangelist, which is OK. Most of the time, however, this order is done out of tradition and religion. Very seldom is a woman accepted as an apostle and her husband as pastor. The Bible says that it is by your fruit that men shall know you (Matt. 7:16) not by your gender; by the gifts and anointing that flows—not whether you are a woman or a man. The problem is not whether or not a man should listen to or agree with a woman making a decision. The point is to agree with God's wisdom—no matter if it is coming from a male or female.

There are times that God gives instructions to a husband, and at other times He gives instructions to the wife. In God, there is neither male nor female (Gal. 3:28). Both men and women must be sensitive to the leading of the Holy Spirit and just obey God, submitting ourselves "one to another in the fear of God" (Eph. 5:21). This is where the kingdom woman begins to break with the traditions of men. We'll discuss in greater detail mutual submission and teamwork between men and women in ministry in upcoming chapters.

Woman of Faith

> Now faith is the substance of things hoped for, the evidence of things not seen.
> —Hebrews 11:1

"Don't let me die with destiny inside of me!" was my constant cry to God during the years I fought one of the hardest battles of my life. It was 1990, and I was constantly being rushed to the hospital because of fainting spells, losing tremendous amounts of blood, and malignant tumors. One tumor was so large I looked like I was five months pregnant. It was the size of a grapefruit, twelve centimeters in diameter. I had been in the hospital almost a month when the doctor scheduled surgery to remove the tumors. It was Thanksgiving weekend. I pleaded with the doctor to let me go home to be with my family. I promised the doctor I would reschedule the surgery, and he agreed to let me go home if I agreed to strict bed rest.

Day and night I prayed, quoting scriptures of healing over my life. Two weeks later I was back at the hospital for the surgery. The doctor wanted to run a test to see if the tumors had grown. When he examined me, he looked puzzled, and said he would be right back. He left me lying there wondering what he found and imagining the worst about how bad it was.

The doctor came back in with another doctor and said, "I want you to look at the test and examine the patient." Then he asked me, "Did you go to another doctor to have the tumor removed?"

I said, "No. I've been at home on bed rest."

He said, "I'm not sure what happened, but the tumor is not there."

I immediately started praising God, "Glory to God for a miraculous miracle!"

He really is the Lord that healed me (Exod. 15:26).

Years later my health was failing again. I was rushed to the hospital and diagnosed with cancer. The doctors wanted to do emergency surgery, but my blood count was too low. They started a blood transfusion, but my body rejected the blood transfusion. I was so weak I could barely whisper. I was in a comatose state, and the doctors told my husband to call my family because they were not sure if I would make it through the night. They also wanted me to sign papers that said if death occurred they would not be responsible.

One of the scriptures I had memorized when I first got saved rushed to my cloudy mind: "I shall not die, but live, and declare the works of the LORD" (Ps. 118:17). I kept repeating it in my head as I laid in the hospital. The Bible says, "As [a man] thinketh in his heart, so is he" (Prov. 23:7), so I was thinking about living.

After some time passed, I was transferred to another hospital. The new doctors said that if I would've had surgery at the other hospital, I might have died on the operating table. The doctor put me on high doses of medication to stabilize me for surgery. I didn't want to have the surgery and I chose to believe God for another supernatural miracle.

I prayed and asked God what to do. The Bible says, "In all thy ways acknowledge him, and he shall direct thy paths" (Prov. 3:6). When I heard the Holy Spirit say, "If thy right arm offend thee, cut it off" (Matt. 5:30), I knew my answer was to trust God through the doctors. Never limit God to just one method of healing. Our ways are not His ways. His thoughts are higher than ours. (See Isaiah 55:8–9.)

I agreed to have the surgery. On January 30, 1995 the cancer was removed, and today I am still cancer free. Glory to God! My faith had increased, and when my sister was diagnosed with cancer, I prayed and believed God for her. Today she is cancer free as well. Cancer runs through our family bloodline. My mother and her sister died from cancer. Kingdom woman, you are a bloodline breaker break the bloodline curse!

If you have a history of sickness and disease in your family, I join my faith with yours and decree and declare that every generational bloodline curse of cancer, tumors, diabetes, high blood pressure, stroke, heart problems, and kidney problems be destroyed by the power of God. If you or someone you know has been diagnosed with cancer, consider what the Bible asks us: "Whose report shall we believe?" The kingdom woman's answer: "I will believe the report of the Lord." Jesus was "wounded for our transgressions, he was bruised for our iniquities: the chastisement of our peace was upon him; and with his stripes we are healed" (Isa. 53:5).

The Bible says, "The thief [Satan] cometh not, but for to steal, and to kill, and to destroy" (John 10:10). The enemy is not only after you, but he also wants your children and family.

Some time ago, my family came under a severe attack with the following events happening within the span of a few weeks. The attacks started by my son being hit by a forklift truck at work. He was rushed to the hospital. He injured his neck, shoulder, and back. The next day my daughter was put into the hospital to have surgery for thyroid cancer. Two days later my sister was admitted into the hospital. She was in a comatose state with high blood pressure. My husband and I went to the hospital to check on her. We both prayed for her, and I stayed at the hospital while my husband went back home.

About two hours later, while I was praying for my sister, I heard someone screaming like I had never heard before. I stopped praying for my sister and began to pray for the person who was in that room, not knowing at the time that it was my husband. I was asking God, "Whoever that person is, please Lord, have mercy. Have mercy, Lord." Minutes later I received a call to come to the hospital because my husband had suffered a massive heart attack. He had been admitted to the hospital and was fighting for his life. I told them that I was already at the hospital. It turned out I was only two rooms away. I went to the room my husband was in and I immediately began praying. I experienced a strength in me that I didn't know I had. My husband was lying there looking lifeless, but I couldn't allow fear to overtake me. I prayed like I never prayed before. I decreed that my husband would not die but live and declare the works of the Lord. It turned out that the doctors had to do emergency surgery on my husband's heart.

After sleeping in the hospital for a week with my husband, I was relieved when the doctors released him to go home. They were amazed at how quickly my husband was recovering. A few months later, my husband returned to the hospital for another surgery on his heart, but today—after those two heart surgeries and four major back surgeries from a previous work injury—he is doing well.

On Thanksgiving Day, during the same season of my life, I had to rush my grandson to the hospital because he was complaining of shortness of breath. A few weeks later, my oldest brother died of cancer. A few months later my mother-in law died. It was challenging, to say the least.

During these difficult seasons I was receiving speaking engagements, but I did not accept the invitations. My first ministry is to my family as a kingdom woman, and to be honest I did not feel like a kingdom woman of faith at all. I felt completely overwhelmed, like the devil was winning and like I had no more strength to fight. All I could say was, "Jesus, help me. Jesus, I need You." The Bible says the God is a very present help in times of trouble (Ps. 46:1). Although I felt overwhelmed in the natural, God gave me a peace that surpasses all understanding. Inwardly I felt a strength that could only come from God. In Zechariah 4:6 it says, "Not by might, nor by power, but by my spirit, saith the Lord of hosts." We must remember when we are faced with adversities we must trust in the strength of the Lord. Psalm 34:19 says, "Many are the afflictions of the righteous: but the Lord delivereth him out of them all." I clung to the Lord, and God spared my husband's life. I claim God's healing by faith. My daughter is healed. My son is healed. My grandson is healed. I thank God for the miracle of His mercy.

There are many things that we will suffer as kingdom women, but God will deliver us from of them all (Ps. 34:19). As you are becoming a woman of faith, you will be faced with many challenges. It's important not to allow fear to get into your heart, but to use those challenges as faith-builders to build your faith. Isaiah 59:19 says, "When the enemy shall come in like a flood, the Spirit of the Lord shall lift up a standard against him." You must not faint in the day of adversity but say, "In the name of Jesus, devil, you will not win, not on my watch." Decree and declare that enough is enough. Let the devil know that he can't have you, he can't have your family, and he can't have your destiny. You are covered by the blood, and no weapon formed against you will prosper.

Let God arise and your enemies be scattered (Ps. 68:1). Let your faith arise and breakthrough, healing, deliverance, salvation, and anything you ask for be done, in the name of Jesus. Kingdom woman, God has given you power to tread upon serpents and scorpions and all the power of the enemy. Greater is He that is in you than he that is in the world. Do not lose sight of the strength and deliverance of God in whatever situation you are facing. Know that He has already won the victory over all the evil that may come against you. Jesus declared,

"Be of good cheer; I have overcome the world" (John 16:33). The enemy may use all kinds of things to get you off track, but let your actions and your prayers show that you walk by faith and not by sight.

Woman of Wisdom

> Wisdom is the principle thing; therefore get wisdom: and with all thy getting get understanding.
> —Proverbs 4:7

You must look to God for wisdom in every area of your life. The Bible says that we need to acknowledge God in all of our ways and He will direct our paths.

There is a danger in not acknowledging God. Without consulting God first in certain situations, you can end up making the wrong decisions, such as marrying the wrong person. Many people have married the wrong person, and they didn't realize it until after they started living together. Some people find out that it was lust and not love. I have heard people say how they went to college to study for a certain degree and later found out that was not what God wanted them to do. Whether it's our work, careers, business decisions, where to live, what church to attend, or even in our giving, it is so important to pray about it, seek God and wait on His answer. Wait on Him to direct your path. I often say this, "No matter what it is you want to do, if there is no peace in it, then it ain't God." However, if we want peace in making decisions we must obey God's will for our life.

Wise and godly people in every age of the world and rank in society agree that true wisdom consists of obedience to the will of God.

How I learned the importance of walking in wisdom

> He shall call upon me, and I will answer him: I will be with him in trouble; I will deliver him, and honour him. With long life will I satisfy him, and show him my salvation.
> —Psalm 91:15–16

One day, when I was working for a school as a crossing guard, a man came and introduced himself as a pastor. He told me his car had broken down and he needed a ride to the bank to cash a check to pay his church's rent. When he got into my car, I received an unction from the Holy Ghost and began to speak in tongues. He went inside the bank and came back out, said that they would not cash the check, and asked me to take him to another bank. I began to speak boldly in warring tongues, and the man jumped out the car and ran down the street.

The next day when I went back to my school crossing guard position, a neighbor said the man that he saw get into my car had just gotten out of jail for murder. The neighbor said he wasn't sure if he would have seen me alive again. I could have been that man's next murder victim.

Your heart may be to help people, but wisdom says in all your ways acknowledge God and He shall direct your steps. You may not always see the enemy for who he is, but God will give His angels to keep watch over you (Ps. 91:11). To use the previous story as an example, from the start, I lacked wisdom by allowing a man that I did not know to get into my car. That neighbor saw a man who wasn't my husband get into my car, which in and of itself did not look good on my part. Secondly, the Bible says not to let your good be evil spoken of (Rom. 14:16). Even without considering this man's potential ill intentions, it was a poor choice. However, because I yielded to the Holy Spirit, my life that could have been put in danger was spared. It is imperative that we acknowledge God in all our ways, and He shall direct our path.

In order to remain under the protection of God's wisdom, kingdom women need to stay in the secret place. (See Psalm 91.) We need to stay hidden in the heart of God, in His Word, in worship, and in His glory. As we abide under His shadow, we will become more sensitive to the Spirit. We will become more discerning of spirits. We will try the spirits by the Spirit to see whether or not they are of God. Never think you can defeat the enemy in your flesh, "for the weapons of our warfare are not carnal, but mighty through God to the pulling down of strong holds" (2 Cor. 10:4).

> A soul without true wisdom and grace is a dead soul. How poor, contemptible, and wretched are, those, who with all their wealth and power, die without getting understanding, without Christ, without hope, and without God!
> —Matthew Henry[3]

Many people chase after wealth, but we can live a wealthy life when we live wisely.

Woman of Wealth

> And when the queen of Sheba heard of the fame of Solomon concerning the name of the Lord, she came to prove him with hard questions. And she came to Jerusalem with a very great train, with

> camels that bare spices, and very much gold, and precious stones: and when she was come to Solomon, she communed with him of all that was in her heart.
>
> —1 Kings 10:1–2

"But thou shalt remember the Lord thy God: for it is he that giveth thee power to get wealth..." (Deut. 8:18). As a kingdom woman, you may have a desire to advance the kingdom by hosting special events in your local church or at other venues. These events can sometimes incur financial expenses. You can trust God to give you power to get wealth to advance the kingdom in this way.

As it was with the Queen of Sheba, a kingdom woman seeks wisdom. She understands that she cannot rule without wisdom. The Bible says, "The fear of the Lord is the beginning of wisdom" (Prov. 9:10), so "get wisdom: and with all thy getting get understanding" (Prov. 4:7). The Queen of Sheba went to King Solomon to satisfy her curiosity. She had heard of his fame and wisdom, so she went to him to receive instruction and wisdom.

The Queen of Sheba apparently had wisdom but wanted to increase in wisdom. The more God increases you with fame, wealth, influence, power, position, and authority, the more you must increase in wisdom and knowledge. To whom much is given, much is required.

The Queen of Sheba came to test King Solomon with riddles and hard questions to see if he was as great as he was reported to be. Not only was she seeking to improve her own wisdom, but also she was religiously inclined. She wanted to know more about the God whom Solomon worshiped and from whom he received his wisdom. She also showed her value of the time Solomon spent sharing his wisdom by rewarding him with gifts. The Bible says,

"Fools despise wisdom" (Prov. 1:7). In other words, the Queen of Sheba was no fool. She knew that even with all her camels, spices, wealth, gold, silver, and precious stones, that if she did not have the wisdom of God she could lose everything.

Along with wealth you must walk in the wisdom of God. A woman of wealth is a woman who God can entrust to be a good steward over what He gives to her. Her wealth is not based on money, material things, or how much she has; but a kingdom woman is wealthy in wisdom. She uses her wealth to be a kingdom distributor: one who has a spirit of generosity, giving to others, helping others, promoting others, blessings others, opening doors for others, empowering others, encouraging others, imparting to others, and mentoring others.

WOMAN OF VALUE

Maybe you grew up in a home where you were being called worthless or stupid. Perhaps you were told you would never be anything. These words often follow us into adulthood and can cause us to devalue ourselves. When we fail to perceive our great worth and feel we don't deserve to be treated well, we become susceptible to entering abusive relationships. Such relationships just perpetuate the cycle by reinforcing the feeling that such treatment is the kind of life we deserve. It is a terrible scenario to marry someone who does not value you.

But value is not conferred by anyone but God. Let me encourage you: the negative words that were spoken over you are not how God defines who you are. The Bible says you have been made in the likeness and the image of God. That means there is greatness inside of you, as well as beauty, glory, and splendor. You are the apple of God's eye. You are valuable in the kingdom. Never put yourself on the clearance or sale rack, for your price is far above rubies (Prov. 31:10).

THE QUALITIES OF A QUEEN

Although *queen* and *woman of value* are two different titles, they both represent the same qualities, worth, morals, and standards. A queen is a woman who rules a country or kingdom that she was born into. She is part of a royal family. She is a woman of value in her domain. A woman of value values the position she has been given. Like a good queen, she will not abuse her position, but she will also value who God has chosen her to be. A woman of value should not lower her standards to be validated by the opinion of others. A queen of quality is not one to look down on others, but rather she reaches down and raises them up to a place of prominence and a place of greatness.

I would like to take this idea of being a queen even further. I love gemstones and often think that as queens, women can display any one of their precious attributes. You may be a diamond queen, a ruby queen, or a pearl queen. Consider the unique characteristics of each of these gemstones and think about the one you resemble the most. The Bible says, "As a man thinks in his heart, so is he" (Prov. 23:7). It's time to think like a queen, act like a queen, and dress like a queen—be a queen.

A diamond queen

A diamond is a pure and extremely hard naturally crystallized stone, a transparent flawless piece of stone especially when cut and polished.[5] It is valued as a precious gem. You've heard the saying, "Diamonds are a girl's best friend." In the natural realm, a diamond is pure and extremely hard. Spiritually, a diamond queen is pure with extreme strength. She cannot be easily broken. She is transparent. When she is cut and polished, she becomes a highly valuable and precious gem.

Diamonds undergo a long process to become what they are. They are exposed to high pressure, heat, and temperatures. Then, once they become diamonds, they are cut to reveal their true beauty. Most women are like diamonds, but not all understand the process they must go through in order to shine. Instead of being willing to submit themselves to the process, they want the very trial that would make them into a diamond to end quickly. However, the process of a kingdom woman is a life journey, and that journey includes pressure. There will be times in your life, diamond queen, when pressure will come to get you and you will be tempted to compromise. Nonetheless, even if the fire gets turned up, you must refuse to compromise godly principles. Like the three Hebrew boys who were thrown into a fiery furnace because they refused to bow to a wicked king, God will preserve you because of your faithfulness. Finally, you must be willing to allow the Lord to cut away your flesh to reveal your full shine. This is symbolic of circumcising the heart. (See Deuteronomy 30:6.) It is imperative that we submit to God, allowing Him to cut away the work of the flesh, such as pride, rebellion, unforgiveness, and anger. We must remember that to be cut is a part of covenant.

A ruby queen

Rubies represent great courage and inner strength. They are blood-red gemstones and are considered to be a leadership stone. Did you know that the ruby is considered the king of the gemstones? A comparison is made between the value of wisdom and rubies. (See Proverbs 31:10.) The price of a virtuous woman is said to be far above rubies. A ruby queen is strong and has great courage and inner strength. She is a blood-red leader who is full of wisdom.

A pearl queen

Just as pearls are made up of layers upon layers, a pearl queen has layers of protection with the whole armor of God. The Bible tells us that a virtuous woman is more precious than jewels. As a jeweler admires and examines every facet of a diamond, ruby, and pearl, so the Lord looks at His daughters. With the same sense, He sees you as His precious jewel. You are His daughter destined for destiny. No matter where you are in life—you may be going through hardships, broken relationships, or health or financial issues—your circumstances do not determine who you are. Adjust your crown, and be the queen God desires you to be.

A Woman of Virtue

When reading Proverbs 31:10–31, many women may feel intimidated by this virtuous standard. They may feel that it is too high to achieve, but we need to see this woman through the eyes of God and not through man. We should stand in agreement with the Word of God that states, "I can do all things through Christ who strengthens me" (Phil. 4:13, NKJV).

If every good and perfect gift comes from God (James 1:17), and those gifts that are placed in us do not operate by might or power but by the Spirit of God (Zech. 4:6), then we need to understand that it is God who gifted this virtuous woman to be a multitasker. He has given her His power to accomplish all that she was tasked to do. It is possible for her to be a wife and mother. She can cook, clean, sew, and work a full-time job. She can have her own business and work in ministry.

The industry and ministry of a virtuous woman strengthens and supports her family. The Bible says, "The heart of her husband safely trusts her" (Prov. 31:11). He has absolute confidence in her faithfulness. He knows she will not waste resources. He is blessed by her tireless industry. He is exalted as a ruler with the elders at the gate. He praises her virtues and her ability to bless others. Even her children rise up and call her blessed (v. 28).

Finis J. Dake points out in the *Dake Annotated Reference Bible* that there are thirty-one characteristics of a virtuous woman.

1. Morally perfect (v. 10)
2. Valuable (v. 10)
3. Trustworthy (v. 11)
4. Good and true (v. 12)
5. Proficient (v. 13)
6. Laborious (v. 14)
7. Considerate (v. 15)
8. Versatile (v. 16)

9. Tireless and healthy (v. 17)
10. Joyful and efficient (v. 18)
11. Watchful and cautious (v. 18)
12. Skillful (v. 19)
13. Merciful (v. 20)
14. Generous (v. 20)
15. Fearless (v. 21)
16. Clever (v. 22)
17. Good taste (v. 22)
18. Respected and popular (v. 23)
19. Industrious and prosperous (v. 24)
20. Dependable and honest (v. 25)
21. Confident (v. 25)
22. Wise (v. 26)
23. Kind and understanding (v. 26)
24. Prudent (v. 27)
25. Energetic (v. 27)
26. Ideal wife and mother (v. 28)
27. Honored by her family (v. 27–28)
28. Excels in virtue (v. 28)
29. God-fearing and humble (v. 30)
30. Successful (v. 31)
31. Honored by the public (v. 31)[6]

I find it very interesting that in this twenty-first century there are still some men and women who think women were only created to be wives and mothers, that they should only cook, clean, help raise the children, and that's all. Some people still tend to think that God only called men to be in positions of power and leadership. No, people of God, this is not what the Bible teaches. It says, "I will pour out My Spirit on all flesh; your sons and your daughters shall prophesy, your old men shall dream dreams, your young men shall see visions" (Joel 2:28).

After reading through this chapter and learning what best describes a Proverbs 31 woman, you may be saying to yourself, "I don't feel like a virtuous woman." You may feel like a failure instead of a woman of faith. You may feel devalued instead of valuable. You may even feel like a victim instead of a victor. But the Lord says, "Behold, I will do a new thing, now it shall spring forth" (Isa. 43:19). I prophesy to you that today is a new day. It's a new season. I prophesy to you a new you. I prophesy that you are a kingdom woman, a Proverbs 31 woman, a wise woman, a confident woman, a successful woman, a prosperous woman, a fearless woman, a woman of honor, and a God-fearing, humble woman.

Now is the time to come out of old mind-sets and put on the mind of Christ. Know that you can be whoever God has created you to be. He will create in you a new heart and a right spirit to be a kingdom woman full of love, ready to go to war for the things He's promised, fruitful and prosperous, faith-filled, bold and courageous, wise, wealthy in both mind and spirit, valuable, and virtuous.

In the next chapter, we will see all of these attributes in motion as we learn the mission of a kingdom woman.

Chapter 3

THE KINGDOM WOMAN ON A MISSION

Go ye into the world and preach the gospel to every creature. He that believeth and is baptized shall be saved; but he that believeth not shall be damned. And these signs shall follow them that believe; in my name shall they cast out devils; they shall speak with new tongues; they shall take up serpents; and if they drink any deadly thing, it shall not hurt them; they shall lay hands on the sick, and they shall recover.
—Mark 16:15–18

Have you ever felt like you are on a mission for God, but the odds are against you? What do you do? It was in the year 2000, and a dear family member's husband went home to be with the Lord. Before he died, he requested that my husband officiate his funeral. My husband then asked me if I would pray at the funeral.

On the day of the funeral, my husband and I walked down the aisle together, side by side. Just before we got ready to go to the pulpit, the pastor of the church stopped us. He said, "She is not allowed in the pulpit. Only men."

My husband told the pastor that I was an ordained prophet and that I would be assisting him with a prayer. The pastor reluctantly said it was OK for me to join my husband in the pulpit.

As I sat there in the pulpit feeling a bit nervous, I could sense a feeling of rejection of women in ministry particularly in the church we were in for the funeral. I could hear in the Spirit that people were saying in their hearts, "What is that woman doing in the pulpit?" I could sense that the members of the church were not pleased that I was sitting in the pulpit. I had a battle going on inside of me: should I obey God or man?

When my husband got up to introduce me, a peace came over me. When I opened my mouth to pray comfort and encourage the family, the power of God filled the atmosphere with glory and power. You could see the look of amazement on the people's faces. They were still clapping their hands after I took my seat.

After the service, the same pastor and several of his deacons who did not want me to sit in the pulpit told me that I did a fantastic job and asked for our ministry information—both mine and my husband's. All the glory belongs to the Lord. I was so thankful to God for pouring out His Spirit upon me and using me as an example. You too will be challenged at times to make a decision to obey God or man.

Several times throughout my ministry, I have been told that women were not allowed in the pulpit. As kingdom women, we must respect a person's church and beliefs. When we understand that the anointing God has put upon our lives will be present wherever we go, it does not matter if we are in the pulpit or in the pews. God's anointing on our lives remains the same. Even if we are surrounded by people who struggle to receive women in ministry, because of the anointing people will not be able to deny our call. It's not us; it's the anointing that breaks and destroys yokes.

Apostle Paul said, "My speech and my preaching was not with enticing words of man's wisdom, but in demonstration of the Spirit and of power" (1 Cor. 2:4).

When God gives you an assignment or a mission, the devil wants you to think that the mission is impossible and there are barriers that you cannot get through or get over to accomplish what God has put before you. As a kingdom woman, it takes courage to be a game changer and break the traditions of men. You may be challenged, criticized, and told you are not allowed to serve in ministry. But God will give you confidence and courage to change the culture you are in. A kingdom woman's heart is to obey God. She knows that obedience is better than sacrifice. Her will is to do the will of the Father. Her cry is "not my will but thy will be done."

My husband and I have studied the example of Aquila and Priscilla. They were a husband-and-wife team who worked in ministry together. Wherever you read about them in the Bible, they are always mentioned together, never separately. They acted as one in all they did. (See Acts 18:26.) I'm not saying that every ministry led by a married person must be co-led with their spouse, but the Bible clearly shows it as one biblical example.

My husband and I do most of our marriage counseling together. Men and women are amazed by our uniqueness and embrace our team ministry. Then there are times when the engaged couple requests that only my husband officiate the wedding. This is not because they are not blessed by me as a woman but, simply out of respect for social and religious customs and traditions, which is OK.

This is one of the main missions I believe the Lord has given kingdom women: to break the traditions of men when it comes to serving God and His people. We must keep in mind that in God, "there is neither male nor female: for ye are all one in Christ Jesus" (Gal. 3:28) and that whom the Lord calls He also qualifies (Rom. 8:30). God will strengthen you to do the things He commands you to do. Although men and women have experienced the power of God in our lives, there are some people who want the anointing but struggle with religious mind-sets of tradition.

Your Kingdom Mandate

In Mark 16:15 Jesus commanded, "Go ye into all the world, and preach the gospel to every creature." Though he articulated this first to His disciples, he intended it for all believers—not just preachers and not just men. As believers, each of us has been given a responsibility to give sinners an invitation to receive Jesus Christ as their Savior. Whether we are male or female, we have been given the same rights, privileges, promises, and provision for service in the kingdom.

What is a mandate? According to Merriam-Webster's dictionary, a mandate is "an authoritative command" or "an authorization to act given to a representative."[1] A mandate can also be an "instruction, directive, decree, command, order…charge, commission…ruling…[or] ordinance.[2] A mandate is "the authority to carry out" an action.[3] A mandate is "a command or authorization to act in a particular way."[4]

It is the responsibility of all believers to go into the world and preach the gospel. The corporate kingdom church has a mandate to gather together for prayer and intercession. The Bible says in Deuteronomy 32:30 that one can chase a thousand, and two can put ten thousand to flight. Apostolic and prophetic corporate mandates are to build and perfect the saints for the work of the ministry, for the edifying of the body of Christ, until we all come into the unity of the faith and of the knowledge of the Son of God (Eph. 4:13).

The kingdom woman's mandate is unique. As an individual you may be given a mandate to be an intercessor. You may have a mandate to become a pastor or a president or a judge. Whatever mandate has been given to you by God, carry it out with power and authority. That will bring glory to God. I was given my kingdom mandate in a dream, which was based on Luke 4:18–19: "The Spirit of the LORD is upon me, because he hath anointed me to preach the gospel to the poor; he hath sent me to heal the brokenhearted, to preach deliverance to the captives, and recovering of sight to the blind, to set at liberty them that are bruised, To preach the acceptable year of the Lord." One of the commands given in Mark 16:15 was to go into all the world. That world may consist of people in your workplace or people in the marketplace. In your neighborhood, community, or at the grocery store, there are people you can reach with the good news of the gospel of Jesus Christ.

A Woman with a Dream and a Vision

> And Joseph dreamed a dream, and he told it to his brethren: and they hated him yet the more.
> —Genesis 37:5

There are so many women who have dreams and visions of becoming wives, mothers, business women, women in ministry, and so much more. According to Merriam-Webster, dreams are "a series of thoughts, images or emotions occurring during sleep." Dreams are sometimes given by God to help you understand what your heavenly calling is while you are on earth. This word can also refer to "a strongly desired goal or purpose."[5]

It is not uncommon for kingdom women to have a dream of doing something big, or something great, or something that has never been done before. Kingdom women are great visionaries. God often gives them insight through dreams and visions. These dreams and visions can be an important part of revealing your destiny. There are times when God will give you prophetic dreams concerning your eternal purpose. By all means, in all thy getting get an understanding about what the dream meant and what instruction God has given you concerning your dream. Pray and ask God to give you the interpretation of your dream, find scripture to confirm your dream, get godly counsel or contact someone that God has gifted in interpreting dreams. There are some people who desire your dream, or desire to do what you do. They may desire the favor you have, your gift or the anointing on your life. You must be very discerning concerning your dreams.

Watch out for dream killers

Satan is a dream killer, and he wants to kill your dreams so that you will not live out your purpose in life. He will use anyone who yields to his trickery to destroy dreams that have come from God. It is imperative that you be led by the Holy Spirit about who you should share your dreams with and when to do this.

Do not share your dreams with dream killers. Do not share your dreams and visions with people who do not have prophetic insight into what God is doing in your life. Do not share your dreams with people who are jealous or envious of you. Joseph's brothers were jealous of him and tried to kill him. Share your dreams with someone who has a gift to interpret dreams and is secure in who they are; watch out for dream killers.

Follow Your Dream

In our modern history, Dr. Martin Luther King Jr. is one who quickly comes to mind when I think of a dreamer. He was known for his famous "I Have a Dream" speech. His dream was to raise the awareness of the public consciousness concerning racism. He wanted to end racial discrimination and segregation in the United States. Dr. King followed his dream, and we now live with many of the benefits of the dream he fought and died for.

In the Bible, there was another dreamer of dreams. His name was Joseph. He had a dream that his brothers would one day bow down and serve him. His dream ultimately got him thrown into a pit and then in prison, but he ended up in the palace. No matter how crazy your dream may seem, follow it. Your dream may be part of your destiny.

In my earlier years I dreamed a lot, just like Joseph. I sensed that there was something different about me. I felt like God wanted to do something special in my life, but I wasn't sure if this was possible. I wasn't sure if God could use me because I wasn't sure God used women. I've had several dreams where I saw myself preaching the gospel and praying for and helping people. I dreamed about being in different countries and nations.

Growing up, I spent hours in my room reading, writing down my dreams or songs given to me by the Holy Spirit—and journaling, filling notebook after notebook. At church, I had this desire to help others but did not have a role model to follow. The women in our church only sang in the choir and cooked chicken dinners on Sunday. Some of my adult friends who were also my childhood friends during this time, often tell me stories of how I used to gather the other kids from our neighborhood to play school and—one of my childhood favorites—church, and I would pretend I was the pastor.

God can use some dreams to confirm what you dreamed in the past and cause them to become a reality in your future. Although I was play-acting as a pastor in my childhood years, I'm now living the experience of pastoring some amazing groups of women, preaching the gospel, and traveling around the world.

Kingdom woman, I encourage you to pray over your dreams, receive prophetic counsel concerning your dreams, ask God to give an interpretation, and follow your dream. Has God called you to pioneer something new or to plant ministries and churches? You may not have ever seen another woman do it, but don't doubt the mandate of God on your life. Don't let your dreams die. Don't let gender keep you out of the game. You may get distracted. You may make some detours. Your destiny may be delayed, but the devil cannot stop or steal the dream that has come from God.

A Woman with a Plan

> For I know the plans that I have for you, saith the LORD, thoughts of peace, and not of evil, to give you an expected end. Then shall ye call upon me and ye shall go and pray unto me, and I will hearken unto you. And ye shall seek me, and find me, when ye shall search for me with all your heart. And I will be found of you, saith the LORD: and I will turn away your captivity, and I will gather you from all the nations, and from all the places whither I have driven you, saith the LORD; and I will bring you again into the place whence I caused you to be carried away captive.
> —JEREMIAH 29:11–14

God has a plan for your life. To discover it, you must be willing to call upon Him, pray, and seek Him. Sometimes you may get carried away by turmoil and trials in your life and the things that hold you captive. For a time, they may carry you away from God's plan, but He says, "I will turn away your captivity." Just like a person who needs direction to get to a certain location, you need God's spiritual GPS plan for you. It's important that you seek Him to discover the plan He has for your life.

As a teenager, I had all these plans of doing something great but wondered how in the world they would happen if I had no parents and no money to go to college. I became angry with God and rebelled. I stopped praying, reading my Bible, and attending church. I felt like an orphan. I felt like I had no purpose for living.

Little did I know God already had a plan for my life. Jeremiah 1:5 says, "Before I formed thee in the belly I knew thee; and before thou camest forth out of the womb I sanctified thee, and I ordained thee a prophet unto the nations." I had not seen any successful, prosperous examples that I could pattern my life after, so the thought that God had a plan in mind for my life seemed impossible. When your life has been full of darkness, it's hard to believe that something good can come out of something that appeared bad as a child. The enemy's job is to get us to doubt God when change doesn't happen right away. But God's time and purpose is different than ours. If there are things you have planned for your life and they do not happen in the time or the way you planned, you may think it wasn't God's will or plan. The Bible says that "the race is not [given] to the swift, nor the battle to the strong" but instead to he who endures to the end (Eccles. 9:11). Endurance will cause you to experience your eternal purpose.

I had plans to go to college, and although I did not go to school to be an X-ray technician, God has given me the gift of discernment. I didn't go to college to become a schoolteacher, but God has given me the grace to teach in the kingdom. I didn't go to college to become a fashion designer, but He gave me the grace to be an entrepreneur. I had hopes of becoming a flight attendant. Instead, God has graced me to travel to different parts of the world—South Africa, Zimbabwe, China, India, Germany, the Bahamas, Florida, California, and Canada. Today I am a wife, mother, grandmother, minister of the gospel, business woman, author, and ambassador.

A woman who plans to use kingdom strategies to overthrow the plots, plans, and schemes of the enemy must also have a plan and strategy for her life. Isaiah 55:8–9 says, "'For my thoughts are not your thoughts, neither are your ways my ways,' saith the LORD. 'For as the heavens are higher than the earth, so are my ways higher than your ways, and my thoughts than your thoughts.'"

Kingdom woman, God has a plan for your life, and you must go through the process to discover it.

A Woman of Destiny

> Verily, verily I say unto you, Except a corn of wheat fall into the ground and die, it abideth alone: but if it die, it bringeth forth much fruit.
> —JOHN 12:24

> Whosoever will come after me, let him deny himself, and take up his cross and follow me
> —MARK 8:34

A woman of destiny dies daily to her flesh. Many talk about living, but very few talk about dying. In order to fulfill your kingdom mandate and discover your destiny, you must be willing to die to self, die to selfish ambition and motives, die to your will, and die to your way.

Could it be that some may not have discovered their destiny because they have refused to yield to the Holy Spirit and die to self? Most people do not know what their destiny is or what God has created them to do. Some people spend all of their lives doing something God never intended for them to do, and sad to say, many people die with their destiny still inside them. Not so for the kingdom woman. The kingdom woman is one who will yield to the Holy Spirit and will deny herself, take up her cross to follow after Christ and her destiny.

One day while I was looking for pictures of my dad for his home-going celebration, I discovered something very startling. I found my mother's obituary in a box. I was a teenager when my mother died of cancer and never paid attention to what was written. This day I looked on the front of my mother's obituary and read, "Someday, if God permits, I would like to preach the gospel and build a church."

This was startling to me because I never knew my mom had plans for her life besides working and taking care of her children. What's even more startling is that we had similar dreams to preach the gospel and build a church. This has been in my heart since I got saved. I think it is very interesting that I have the same desire my mom had. She did not talk much about her life, but my other siblings shared stories about my mom and how she traveled as a singer and worked with celebrities in her early years.

I am reminded of the times when I was a little girl and my family was together, we would take long drives after church into beautiful neighborhoods looking at beautiful homes while I was sitting in the back seat of the car. I was fascinated with looking at beautiful homes and buildings, imagining that one day I would build my own house and maybe even build a church. I just imagined that I would build something great one day but growing up on welfare and in poverty made that dream seem impossible. What seems impossible, God made possible. When we embrace becoming a kingdom woman, God can change our status from rags to riches. I love that God has partially fulfilled this dream: I had the opportunity to design and build the house I live in now.

God's eternal purpose for you is that, even after you are dead and gone, your eternal purpose will live on—whether it's through your children, work you've done, lives you have touched, or books you have written. God's purpose for your life will live on forever so that the generations to come will be blessed by the life you lived.

A woman of destiny will follow the plans of God for her life. Our plans may not always go the way we think, for our ways are not His ways. His ways are higher than our ways. I'm still amazed that my mom's mantle fell on me. God has graced me to preached the gospel, sing prophetically, and build spiritually. My mom died too soon and did not fulfill her dreams, but the Bible says that all things work together for our good (Rom. 8:28). In so many ways I feel like I'm walking in my mother's shoes. What better plan and destiny could I be living as a kingdom woman than the one God began with my mother?

Are You Qualified?

Growing up with five brothers, I wanted to do whatever they did. The problem was they did not think I was qualified. When it came to playing sports, my brothers didn't want me to play with them because I was a girl. Even though my brothers saw that I could do some of the things they could do like play basketball, baseball, marbles, climb trees, and ride a bicycle on one wheel, they still did not want me to participate in their activities.

One day my brothers and friends did not have enough players for their baseball game. Seeing that they needed one more player to complete their team, I asked them if I could play. Reluctantly they said yes. We won the game and from that day on my brothers did not just see me as their little sister but as someone who could help them win.

This same behavior has gone on in the body of Christ. You may not be invited to be part of some teams, groups, and cliques based on people's personal opinions. But a kingdom woman will invite you to be a part of her team because she understands there is one true faith, one Lord, one baptism, and we are all on the same team. The apostle Paul said in Philippians 3:14, "I press on toward the goal to win the [heavenly] prize of the upward call of God in Christ Jesus." Together, we win.

The enemy comes to plant seeds of doubt in your heart at an early age, making you feel that you are not qualified based on your gender. Through rejection, he waters these seeds with a lack of confidence—one of many dream killers. Don't allow the enemy to kill your God-given dreams.

Being a female does not automatically sideline or limit you. If God has called you to do a special work, He will give you the grace to govern the gift inside of you and the favor to find the place where it is to be shared and received.

I personally believe there are some things that are off-limits to a female. Being a woman does not limit your call; however, there should be a difference between a woman's mannerisms and a man's. There should be a clear distinction between male or female. Although men and women are equal in God's eyes, women should not try to compete with or preach like men or display masculinity like men. A woman should be soft by nature and feminine but powerful in God. I love being a female—a princess and daughter of the sovereign King, dressed in dignity for divine destiny.

Break the Spirit of Tradition

All traditions aren't bad. The early church was founded on tradition and religion. Some traditions, however, can become outdated and can need an upgrade. Back in the day, women were only allowed to teach Sunday School, sing in the choir, and cook chicken dinners.

Kingdom woman, dream bigger than just those roles. See yourself doing more than teaching Sunday school, singing in the choir, or cooking chicken dinners. Although these are the roles that man has tried to limit women to—and we are influential and gifted in these areas —God has always had many different gifts and assignments to give to His kingdom women. If we are gifted in teaching and hospitality gifts we need to pursue them with all our might as unto the Lord, and if God has shown us other less traditional roles, we need to pursue Him so that He may reveal to us all that He has planned.

God can send you to the nations. He can use you to preach the gospel and to be a pastor. He can appoint you to be a mentor and raise up other women and empower them in ministry. God can use you in the marketplace or give you your own business. God can use you like He did Esther to bring deliverance to her people. It is time to break the spirit of tradition and declare, "My dreams are getting bigger!"

As a woman on a mission, there will be obstacles you will run across, but you must obey God who has called you for such a time as this. You cannot be a man pleaser; you must seek to be a God pleaser. The Bible teaches that "we ought to obey God rather than men" (Acts 5:29).

Kingdom women are game changers. They will not stay stuck in tradition and religion. They will oppose the odds against them and obey the assignment given to them by God.

Chapter 4

THE KINGDOM WOMAN—TESTED AND PROVEN, DELIVERED AND SET FREE

But he knoweth the way that I take: when he hath tried me, I shall come forth as pure gold.
—Job 23:10

J<small>UST AS GOLD</small> must be tried in the fire and tested and proven, you too must be tried in the fire and tested and proven. I often say people want the platform without the process. When God begins the process to make you into a kingdom woman, everything in your life will be tested. Your family, marriage, finances, friendships, gifts, love, mind, motives, and even your health will be tested. Everything must be tested, tried, and proven. Why? You may have heard this phase, "no one likes bread half-baked." Well, neither does God. God loves you too much to release you before it's time. He knows that people would much rather listen to someone who has gone through the process—someone with an experience and an overcoming testimony. So don't run away from the fire, but allow the fire to burn out everything that's in you that is not like God. Allow God to give you a spiritual makeover.

We live in a day and age when natural, physical makeovers are in demand—facials, new makeup, cosmetic surgery, and so on—all to create a whole new, more vibrant and beautiful look. We need to have the same thing happen spiritually. It's time for the twenty-first century church to get a makeover.

Despite all the controversy over women being in positions of authority as pastors or apostles, we must understand we are living in the twenty-first century. We need a church makeover. Many would rather stay stuck in traditions and religion with old wineskins, but the shift has already taken place in the apostolic culture with apostolic women. It's time that we accept the makeover God has for the body of Christ. We must be willing to let God put us on His potter's wheel and make us virtuous vessels fit for His use.

Arise, and Go Down to the Potter's House

> The word which came to Jeremiah from the LORD, saying, Arise, and go down to the potter's house, and there I will cause thee to hear my words. Then I went down to the potter's house, and, behold, he wrought a work on the wheels. And the vessel that he made of clay was marred in the hand of the potter: so he made it again another vessel, as seemed good to the potter to make it. Then the word of the LORD came to me, saying, O house of

Israel, cannot I do with you as this potter? saith the LORD.

—JEREMIAH 18:1–6

God told Jeremiah, "Up on your feet! Go to the potter's house. When you get there, I'll tell you what I have to say." So I went to the potter's house, and sure enough, the potter was there, working away at his wheel. Whenever the pot the potter was working on turned out badly, as sometimes happens when you are working with clay, the potter would simply start over and use the same clay to make another pot. Then GOD's Message came to me: "Can't I just do as this potter does, people of Israel?"

—JEREMIAH 18:1–6, THE MESSAGE

When a vessel was marred or did not turn out according to the original plan, it was not thrown away. Instead, the clay was crushed and returned to the wheel, and it was made over again. This continued until the clay took on the shape that the potter intended for it to be. This is what God declared He had the power to do with Israel.

You may have been marred or scarred, or some of you were messed up––but God will not throw you away. The Lord told the prophet Jeremiah, "Get up on your feet." In other words, He was saying to him, "Arise and come to the Potter's house. Come to Me. Get into My presence, and when you get in My presence, I will tell you how messed up you are." It takes God to show us what state we are in, because sometimes we have a tendency to think we are all right. But the Bible says, "There is a way which seemeth right unto a man, but the end thereof are the ways of death" (Prov. 14:12).

God's Spiritual Makeover

You must go to God and allow Him to do a deep work on the inside. This means you allow God to deal with the sins and the issues in your heart. It also means you allow God to take away any hurts, fears, rejection, pride, and unforgiveness. These things hinder your growth. The Lord loves you too much to leave you in a broken state. Things in your life may have turned out badly, but just know what the devil meant for bad, God can turn for your good (Gen. 50:20). Arise and go down to the Potter's house!

The Lord is saying, "Can't I just do as I please with you?" (See Jeremiah 18:6.)

Don't allow the devil to cause you to throw away your dreams and visions. God has a destiny for you. He is remaking, reshaping, remolding, relaunching, and resetting you. Remember, even if you are imperfect, the Potter will not throw you away but will keep working on you.

God is going to give you your identity back. He is saying to you today, "Get up and go to the Potter's house."

Sometimes when you are going through tough times, the devil wants you to get depressed. But no, you need to get up like God told Jeremiah and go to the house of the Lord. David said, "I was glad when they said unto me, Let us go into the house of the LORD" (Ps. 122:1).

God is going to give you your peace back. He is going to give you your joy and victory back. Don't allow the enemy to tell you otherwise.

After God brings us through, it is important that we do not forget His work in us so that we won't throw away those we minister to who have been marred and scarred. We should not look down on those who have struggles or who are in a place of darkness. Apostle Paul said, "And such were some of you" (1 Cor. 6:11).

We must pray for them to be delivered and see God's full potential that is inside of them completely developed. They may not look like you or dress like you, but just love them and let God make them into His likeness (Gen. 1:27).

God's spiritual makeover is to work out your imperfections and turn you into something that benefits the kingdom. Many women, through life circumstances, may have had it hard. They may have grown up in a dysfunctional environment with drinking, drugs, abuse, violence and molestation. Many have been involved in fornication, adultery, prostitution, lesbian lifestyles, and divorce. Many have been hurt and misunderstood, and as a result have suffered from rejection.

Many women have lost their dignity, divine quality, value, honor, glory, splendor, self-esteem, courage, beauty, strength, identity, and authenticity. It makes no difference what they have been through in life. God has created them for His glory. When a kingdom woman submits herself to His process on the Potter's wheel, she will come out as a powerful woman ready to accept the call and do the will of the King.

The Gift of Resilience

> For I reckon that the sufferings of this present time are not worthy to be compared with the glory that is to be revealed.
> —Romans 8:18

The word *resilience* means to have "the capacity to recover quickly from difficulties," hard or tough situations.[1]

There will be times that a kingdom woman will suffer some things for the sake of Christ, but the scripture says that this suffering is not worthy to be compared with the glory that shall be revealed (Rom. 8:18). A resilient woman will recover from the difficult, tough, and hard sufferings that she may go through in her life. A woman of resilience has the capacity to recover quickly from difficulties. She is tough.

I am the sixth of eight children. My mother was a single parent through most of her child-rearing years. She struggled to take care of her first five children, so when she became pregnant with me, the thought of having a sixth child was unbearable. My mom—being young, scared, and discouraged—tried to abort me.

Being rejected while I was in my mother's womb opened the door for spirits of rejection. I struggled with rejection growing up. Many people had teenage or young mothers who did not have the resiliency needed to raise their children. As a result, those mothers felt pressured to either abort their baby or give their baby to the grandmother to bring up. It's not that my mother didn't want me, she just didn't know how she was going to feed another child. Thankfully, God intervened and birthed me into the earth for such a time as this (Esther 4:14). God has a purpose for everything we go through in life.

You Can Recover from Difficulties

God begins the process of developing resiliency early in your life. Resiliency helps you to recover from difficulties and setbacks.

Many people go into ministry unaware of the battles

ahead. God oftentimes takes you through the process before He puts you on the platform. I had no idea that all of the pain I went through growing up would prepare me for my purpose in ministry today.

I was only sixteen when my mom was diagnosed with lung cancer. Can you imagine the fear that gripped me when I found out? My mom had surgery, but the cancer still spread throughout her body and she was sent home to receive hospice care.

I became the caretaker for my mom. Every morning before leaving for school I would bathe her, comb her hair, feed her, read scriptures to her, anoint her with oil, and pray for her. I would tell her, "Mom, God is going to heal you." This may seem like an unlikely thing for a teenager to do, but my mom taught us to pray at a very young age. God would also give me songs to sing. I didn't know it at that time, but they were prophetic songs from the Lord.

Becoming a caretaker for my mom taught me how to have compassion for the hurting and how to pray for the sick. A kingdom woman has the compassion for the lost and hurting and must be willing to pray and help them in their time of need. Some people like to be seen with power on a public platform, but God wants to see how well we do with power in private. God was teaching me in private how to activate my prayer life even as a teenager.

When the Lord showed me in a dream that my mom was going home to be with Him, it was difficult to accept. Although we grew up in the church, after my mom died of cancer I turned away from God. At the age of seventeen, I didn't understand why God would take away the only person who was there to protect me and provide for me. My mom was the one I talked to about my dreams, visions, hopes, desires, and deepest thoughts. I didn't understand why I was left here on Earth as a teenager without my mother and with a father whom no one could locate at the time.

Depression

As years went by, I became very depressed. I would come home from school and sit in the closet for hours, crying for God to take me to heaven to be with my mom. The depression was so bad I shut down and wouldn't talk to anyone. I stayed in my room with the door closed, and to end the pain I attempted suicide.

I was taken to the hospital and was treated with therapy. I felt abandoned, rejected, and afraid. I suffered both emotionally and mentally so much that all I could do was cry out to God for help. It was difficult for me at the age of seventeen having to take on the responsibility of becoming an adult and looking after my younger siblings. I was left to fend for myself as a young girl. I remember being terrified, and not knowing how I was going to survive. I went to bed hungry many nights, and cried myself to sleep. I had no one to turn to or to talk to, so I just suffered in silence.

I would ask myself the question repeatedly in my mind, "What have I done to deserve this kind of life? Why can't I have a normal life like any other teenager?" The truth of the matter is that no one's life is perfect, and we really don't know what others go through in life. Each one of us has our own cross to carry. The Bible says, "And we know all things work together for good to them that love God, to them who are called according to His purpose" (Rom. 8:28).

On April 16, 1976, when I was seventeen years old and still in high school, I got married. I did not pray or seek God concerning my marriage as the Bible instruct us to do. Matthew 6:33 says, "Seek ye first the kingdom of God, and his righteousness; and all these things shall be added unto you." But I just decided to get married because my husband wouldn't take no for an answer. He was determined not to abandon me and our baby after he got me pregnant, like his dad abandoned him. He continued to visit me and take me out on dinner dates. He even helped me with taking care of my younger siblings. I was really impressed by that. Most of all, he continued to demonstrate his love for me. After we got married, we got a small apartment and started raising our family. My husband never wanted me to work. He wanted to assure me that he could provide for his family, but we were barely making ends meet. I remember we had to use baking soda to brush our teeth and as deodorant. I was tired of living like that, so I went against his will and got a job.

Although we didn't have all of the necessities, the first three years of marriage seemed like a fairy tale. The reason I said our marriage seemed like a fairy tale is because I remember hearing stories from older women I worked with, about the horrible adulterous and abusive marriages they were in. The women would come to work and talk about the fights and arguments they had with their spouses. Hearing about these abusive marriages on a daily basis as a teenage wife, I began to think my fairytale marriage that did not involve arguments, adultery, fighting, drinking, or drugs at that time seemed too good to be true. Little did I know that, the horrible things I heard about at work with women in their marriage, would later become my own story. I became a victim of those same offenses and lived the next seven years in my worst nightmare.

My job gave us extra money, but our marriage began to fall apart. My husband worked day shift. I worked night shift because that was the only shift that was available at the time. My husband was very angry at me because I got a job against his wishes. He felt it made him feel less than a man. We had very little conversation or time together. I watched the children during the day; he watched the children at night. When I was coming home from night shift, he was standing at the door waiting to leave out for day shift. Although I made sure the apartment was clean, dinner was cooked, and children were bathed, my husband still seemed to be unhappy.

I first noticed that he started drinking when I left my night shift job early. I was excited about spending the evening with my husband and children. Sadly, I came home to find my husband asleep on the couch with the smell of alcohol on his breath, and my baby girl completely covered with Vaseline. My husband denied that he had been drinking. For the sake of peace, I cleaned my daughter up and went to bed. Months later, I started to notice my husband drinking began to increase. I also found drugs in his pocket.

Years later, I found out that he was also committing adultery. This behavior caused arguments and years of verbal, physical, and mental and emotional abuse. The devil convinced me that my husband's drinking, drugs, and adulterous affairs were all my fault. I reasoned that none of this would have happened if I hadn't started working. For years, I blamed myself for my marriage falling apart. The truth of the matter was that drinking, drugs, and adultery were apart of my husband's bloodline and background. I just didn't want to believe that these things would affect my marriage. I saw signs but I ignored them, thinking that if I prayed and fasted long enough my husband would stop and we could have the fairytale marriage we once had. Needless to say, that was the furthest from the truth. It seemed like the more I prayed the worst things got. My husband moved out and left me and my four children for another woman. The pain was so great that once again I tried to commit suicide. This time I found myself in the hospital in the psych ward.

Wrong diagnosis

Some doctors assume a person is crazy if they are placed in the psych ward, but that's not always the case. There are so many people who are suffering silently with manic depression. The truth is, the enemy does not want you to think you have been created to be a kingdom woman. Instead, he wants you to feel that your life does not matter.

Manic depression can lead to suicidal thoughts. I knew I wasn't crazy, but I felt like I had no purpose for living. The only one who could help me was God, and I had turned away from Him. I refused to take the drugs the doctors gave me.

I remember looking up toward heaven and crying out to God saying, "Lord, please get me out of here. I know I'm not crazy. Lord, if You get me out of here, I promise I will serve You and live for You the rest of my life."

How many of you prayed that same prayer? You may relate to Jonah, who ran from God and found himself in the belly of a whale.

I believe God ordained our marriage and therefore was obligated to help us through the process. God did His part, but now it was time for me to hold up my end of the deal. On April 27, 1980, I rededicated my life to the Lord. I went back to church and started reading my Bible, fasting, and praying. After all that, I was surprised to see that the same fears I had growing up were still there.

By this time, my husband had also started going to church, but his behavior did not change right away. He was still smoking, drinking, and doing drugs. Sometimes we are aware of these addictions but somehow think we can change our spouses after we get married.

It is so important for you to wait on the spouse God has ordained for you, because the process is very painful if you don't. Many times the relationship ends in divorce, leaving you feeling rejected, bitter, angry, and abandoned. I was trying to help my husband get set free, but I was not free. Even when a marriage or relationship is ordained by God, you will go through times of testing. "But he knoweth the way that I take: when he hath tried me, I shall come forth as gold" (Job 23:10).

Rejection

As I stated earlier, all of my life I struggled with the spirit of rejection. I often asked God, What is wrong with me? Why do I feel rejected? Why do I feel like I don't fit in anywhere? I thought it was because I was an introvert. Years later in my adult age, I discovered the problem was not because I was an introvert but the root of rejection that had started to develop in me while I was in my mother's womb. Little did I know that this led to self-rejection and the fear of rejection. A kingdom woman may experience rejection time and time again but can and will overcome it through deliverance.

I write with tears in my eyes as I think of all the years rejection ruled my life. Rejection can make you feel like no one loves you and it can make you feel disconnected from the body of Christ. Although you may sense the call of God upon your life, you will not pursue destiny, because you are afraid that people will reject you. This is a major problem for many believers in the body of Christ, and it can hinder them from moving forward.

In my own experience, there were times when the enemy got in and made me doubt I had a purpose, but for the most part I had no one to blame but myself for the years I believed his lies. I believed that no one loved me and that I did not fit in. The enemy uses rejection to ruin relationships.

Can you imagine going through life not being accepted? You feel overlooked, lonely, and outcast. You feel like a person with leprosy—unloved and unwanted. Even though in your heart you may love God, you won't connect well with others if you fear rejection. Rejection robs you of receiving what rightfully belongs to you.

Revelation about rejection will release restoration

My former pastor, Apostle John Eckhardt, wrote a book called *Destroying the Spirit of Rejection*. Although I had read other books on rejection and had gone through deliverance from rejection, while reading his book, I found myself weeping over some relationships. I loved deeply but always felt rejected.

It's important to receive deliverance on a consistent basis. Things happen in our lives unexpectedly and can leave us feeling rejected. Kingdom woman, it's your responsibility to stay free from spirits of rejection, fear of rejection, and self-rejection. You can't help someone else get free if you are not set free.

Rejection hinders the inability to receive or give love and can manifest in the following ways:

- Rejection can cause you to believe that other people do not love you.
- Rejection can ruin relationships.
- Rejection can cause you not to have relationships with people you love.
- Rejection can cause others to reject you.
- Rejection can cause others not to embrace you.
- Rejection can cause you to be overlooked.
- Rejection can close doors and opportunities in ministry.
- Rejection can stop you from moving forward in ministry at all and can cause you to not go after things you desire.

The root of rejection almost ruined my life, but God rescued, delivered, and restored me. You may think that rejection has ruined your life, but God is a God of restoration. He can and will "restore the years that the locust hath eaten, the cankerworm, and the caterpillar and the palmerworm" (Joel 2:25).

God will give you the capacity to become resilient and to recover from difficulties, rejection, self-rejection, and the very fear of rejection. If you are tired of the spirit of rejection ruining your life, make the decision to receive deliverance from it. Arise, lay the axe at the root of rejection, bind, renounce, cast out, and cut off rejection. Reject rejection and decree and declare it will no longer ruin your life.

Religious Bullies

The enemy seeks to pursue the righteous, but a kingdom woman is as bold as a lion (Prov. 28:1). Growing up in school, I had to deal with being bullied almost every day. These bullies had mistaken my quietness and shyness for something totally different. They thought I believed I was too good to be their friend, but that was the furthest thing from the truth.

In reality I was a loner and introvert who lacked social communication skills and was too afraid to approach them. I was afraid of being rejected, so I just stayed to myself. I often ran home to keep the girls from attacking me. I was known as a peacemaker. In fact I would invite some of those same bullies that wanted fight me to come over to my house after school to jump rope. My sisters had no problem dealing with bullies and often fought my bullies for me.

Surprisingly, I never thought that I would have to deal with bullies in the church, but there are spiritual bullies in the church. They see your potential and try to intimidate you by refusing to embrace you, speak to you, or allow you into their circle. They may even go to the pastors and leaders of the church to put thoughts of suspicion in their minds about you with the intent of building trust in the pastor concerning them while causing the pastor and leaders to have mistrust towards you. I've not only seen this happen to others, I have personally experienced this in my own life. The purpose of this kind of behavior from spiritual bullies is to maintain their turf from any new kids on the block.

Bullies are very territorial; that's how bullies operate they develop a group or gang. In the natural, if you came on a street gang's turf or territory, you were threatened, intimidated, beaten, and in some cases people have lost their lives. Bullying should never be taken lightly rather natural bullying or spiritual bullying. Some parents have lost children to bullies. Some spiritual parents have lost spiritual children to spiritual bullies. They either move to another school or neighborhood, or they leave and go find another church.

I believe most people have experienced at least one bully in their life. The minute you join a church, religious bullies are used by the enemy to target you. They size you up and find something they don't like about you. Most of the time, religious bullies are intimidated by you and the anointing that is on your life. Church bullies feel as if you are a threat to them or their positions.

Religious bullies may use scare tactics like slander and gossip to turn others against you. People who are bullies are insecure within themselves but will bully others to try to gain self-esteem.

These are spirits sent on assignment to be distractions. A kingdom woman is not taken down by church bullies. She prays for breakthrough that will change the climate of the church.

David was faced with a bully by the name of Goliath, but God gave him a strategy to overcome his bully. David, the shepherd boy, killed the lion and the bear. Goliath bullied David, but David was not afraid. He said:

> Who is this uncircumcised Philistine, that he should defy the armies of the living God?...Then said David to the Philistine, Thou comest to me with a sword, and with a spear, and with a shield: but I come to thee in the name of the LORD of hosts, the God of the armies of Israel, whom thou hast defied.
>
> This day will the LORD deliver thee into mine hand; and I will smite thee, and take thine head from thee; and I will give the carcases of the host of the Philistines this day unto the fowls of the air, and to the wild beasts of the earth; that all the earth may know that there is a God in Israel."
> —1 SAMUEL 17:26, 45–46

A kingdom woman is as bold as a lion. When her enemies rise up against her, she releases a lioness roar that will cause them to flee. There are religious bullies who will always come to challenge you through mocking, gossiping, backbiting, sabotage, making secret conspiracies, and character assassination. Religious bullies may gang up on you, but you have to become like David in the Spirit and say, "Who is this uncircumcised Philistine, that he should defy the armies of the living God?" (1 Sam. 17:26). Who are these religious bullies who want to shut up the kingdom from you? Don't allow bullies, fear of man, rejection, or any other thing to stop you from walking in purpose and destiny. Kingdom woman, you must learn how to deal with the bullies in your life. You cannot be a coward. You must become a champion.

Fear

> God hath not given us the spirit of fear; but of power, and of love, and of a sound mind.
> —2 Timothy 1:7

Fear does not come from God. God will train you to become a kingdom woman who fights the good fight of faith. The Bible says that we don't wrestle against flesh and blood, but against principalities, powers, rulers of darkness, and spiritual wickedness in high places.

There was this one particular girl whose entire family was full of bullies and gang bangers. They carried knives and guns. Nobody messed with them. Everyone was afraid of them, including me. On the last day of my senior year in high school, she told the other schoolmates she was going to fight me after school.

I was so afraid that I told the teacher I was not feeling well and asked to leave a few minutes before the bell rang. The teacher said yes. As I was walking home, the girl ran up behind me and started pulling my hair out and punching me from the back. Before I realized anything, I picked up a rock and hit her hard as I could.

Blood was everywhere. I didn't know until much later that the impact of the rock I threw at her caused her to go to the hospital to get several stitches. God knows I didn't mean to hurt her, but I will say this, that was the last time she or any other girl tried to bully me ever again.

The enemy wants to bully you, but God will give you

the boldness you need to defeat your enemies. From that day on my sisters did not have to fight for me. In fact, they now call on me to help fight their spiritual battles. The Bible says that "we wrestle not against flesh and blood, but against principalities, against powers, against the rulers of the darkness of this world, against spiritual wickedness in high places" (Eph. 6:12).

There are two kinds of fears: the fear of the Lord and a demonic fear that comes from Satan. When you do not know who you are in the Lord, fear can paralyze you. Fear restricts, torments, and can even stop you from obeying God. The Bible says, "Perfect love casteth out fear" (1 John 4:18). We can overcome fear by perfecting our love for God, and we can develop the kind of love that overcomes fear by choosing to love others unconditionally.

How does fear enter someone's life?

I believe fear entered me while I was in my mother's womb—the fear of dying when my mom tried to abort me. I lived with the fear of dying prematurely. I had crazy dreams about death, and whenever I became very sick I feared dying prematurely. The fear grew stronger after realizing that the women in our family all died in their forties. I saw my mom die prematurely at the age of forty-nine, and I feared that I would not live to see the age fifty.

Fear is not something that goes away on its own. You must face your fears. You must decree with your mouth. You must keep in mind that God has not given you the spirit of fear but one of power, love, and a sound mind, and that no weapon formed against you shall prosper (2 Tim. 1:7; Isa. 54:17).

Generational Curses

> Christ hath redeemed us from the curse of the law, being made a curse for us.
> —Galatians 3:13

Christian marriages and families come under spiritual attack, and they may not be aware of what is going on. The Bible says that Satan walks about like a roaring lion seeking whom he may devour (1 Pet. 5:8). A kingdom woman must be trained in spiritual warfare and learn how to combat the enemy. Although Christ has redeemed us from the curse of the Law, demonic spirits violate the Law. Therefore, you must use your authority to break the curse that comes to hinder you from walking in your divine destiny. God is raising up women generals in this hour to take back what rightfully belongs to them and their families and to confront generational curses.

Have you ever wondered how it is that in some families all the women have had cancer or that all the men are addicted to alcohol? Have you seen some families that have suffered generation after generation of incest and molestation? Maybe you've noticed similar curses in your own family. Pray and ask God to give you strategies to break these curses.

Can a curse affect you?

The Bible says, "So the curse causeless shall not come" (Prov. 26:2). A causeless curse is that which is uttered against one who has done nothing to deserve it. Although you may have done nothing wrong, a curse can still come down through your bloodline and affect you. Have you seen families struggle with poverty from one generation to the next? Have you seen premature death in various generations? These are generational curses. Generational curses are the result of the sins of the fathers visiting the third and fourth generation. (See Exodus 20:5.) This may not pertain to everyone. Your situation may be different, but bloodline generational curses still exist.

It may seem unfair to punish children for their fathers' sins. It's not that God was trying to punish the children. It's just that the effects of sin are naturally passed down from one generation to the next. But thankfully, God can break every one of those curses off our lives.

While I was in the hospital for weeks, the doctors told me there was a possibility I would not make it through the night. My husband was told to contact my family. Thank God I survived cancer. I then had a stroke and lost some of my memory and speech ability, but thank God I survived.

God spared my life in two car accidents. A car hit me when I worked as a school crossing guard. I suffered a concussion and nerve damage, but I am thankful to God that the generational curse of premature death has been broken off my life. I am an overcomer.

Jesus Christ died on the cross and shed His blood so that we could be redeemed from the curse of the Law. Generational curses are broken through salvation, deliverance, and obedience to God's Word.

On December 19, 2017, I celebrated sixty years of life. I say this as a testimony to the glory of God. I truly feared for years that I was going to die in my forties, but God preserved my life for such a time as this. As the scripture says, "Yea, though I walk through the valley of the shadow of death, I shall fear no evil: for thou art with me" (Ps. 23:4). Kingdom women walk in faith, not in fear. Isaiah 54:17 is true: "No weapon formed against you shall prosper."

The Bible says that "Satan comes to steal, kill, and destroy" (John 10:10). The enemy uses different devices to try to destroy you, and he begins his work against the call on your life when you are at an early age.

My mom never discussed this with me, but I believe my mom was abused and molested. I was abused and molested. My daughter was abused and molested. With us, that makes our third and fourth generation.

Second Corinthians 2:11 warns us not to be ignorant of Satan's devices. The devil targets us to destroy our destinies.

I believe I was five years old when my dad left home. As a result, my mom began working long nights, but she didn't make enough money to make ends meets, so our family had to move in with another family. This was an open door for the enemy to use family members to molest me. They would threaten to have their friends beat me up if I told anyone.

I wanted to tell my mom what was going on, but the thought of doing so tormented my little mind. The devil told me if I told my mom I would cause the whole family to be put out on the streets. Our family had been evicted several times with all our furniture and clothing on the streets. I did not want that to happen again. So what did I do? I held this painful secret to myself and suffered in silence.

Thank God we eventually moved out of that abusive home. The family member who molested me as a child is now deceased, but I had the privilege of witnessing to that person before they died.

The devil may have taken advantage of you and robbed you of your innocence. You may have been molested, raped, or experienced other types of trauma in your early years, but God can still do something great in your life. The enemy wants to hold you in a spiritual prison. He wants you to hold on to unforgiveness. But God wants you to walk in freedom, healing, and wholeness. I've talked to women who are angry and bitter at the people who hurt or harmed them. They are also angry and bitter at God, thinking He allowed these things to happen. You must be willing to forgive everyone including yourself. If you refuse to forgive, you will hinder the fulfillment of God's plan for your life. Forgiveness may take time, but it's imperative to your own healing and deliverance. Forgiveness is necessary if you want to break generational curses.

The Bible says that Satan comes to steal, kill, and destroy, but Jesus came that we might have life and life more abundantly (John 10:10). I decree abundant life over you. I decree you shall not die but live and declare the works of Jesus (Ps. 118:17).

> But ye are a chosen generation, a royal priesthood an holy nation, a peculiar people; that ye should shew forth the praises of him who hath called you out of darkness into his marvellous light.
> —1 Peter 2:9

Steps to breaking generational curses

1. Receive salvation by confessing Jesus Christ as Lord

2. Repent of your sins and the sins of your ancestors
3. Obey God's Word and live a holy life
4. Take authority and verbally break repeated generational curses
5. Forgiveness is a key to Freedom

If you have experienced generational curses, I want you to know that you are not alone. Know that you are not to blame. Most importantly, know that you are not the victim but the victor in Christ, because God can take your pain and turn it into the power to encourage, educate, and empower others. Don't stay stuck in the pain of your past. Arise from that broken place and embrace the God of your breakthrough. Break the generational curse and become the kingdom woman God has destined you to be.

Woman of Deliverance

> But upon mount Zion shall be deliverance and there shall be holiness; and the house of Jacob shall possess their possessions.
> —Obadiah 1:17

In the natural world, there are female doctors and midwives who help deliver thousands of babies. The same thing is happening in the spiritual world. God is raising up women who will help birth others and set captives free. These women have been delivered from strongholds and are walking in holiness. They have learned how to possess what God said they can have. There is a fresh anointing being released upon spiritual deliverers to help set others free. Deliverance is the children's bread and we must continually cry out to God to deliver us (Matt. 15:26).

We are three-part beings—spirit, soul, and body. We have a spirit that has a soul and lives in a body. Our spirit is saved at the time of salvation according to 1 Corinthians 2:11–16, but our souls go through a process of deliverance (Gal. 5:17). This is why the Bible says work out your own salvation (or deliverance) as we live day by day. We ought to die daily to our flesh or soul (Phil. 2:12). Our bodies are what we present "as a living sacrifice holy and acceptable to God; which is your reasonable service" (Rom. 12:1–2).

A kingdom woman must be desperate about deliverance and does not allow demons to dictate her destiny.

Forgiveness: A Key to Freedom

> But if ye forgive not men their trespasses, neither will your Father forgive your trespasses.
> —Matthew 6:15

> Then Peter came to Jesus and asked, "Lord, how many times shall I forgive my brother or sister who sins against me? Up to seven times?" Jesus answered, "I tell you, not seven times, but seventy-seven times.
> —Matthew 18:21–22, niv

You must be willing to forgive yourself for the mistakes you made and forgive others for things they did wrong. The Lord had given my husband a breakthrough. For months, he had stopped smoking, drinking, doing drugs, and chasing women. One night he decided to go bowling with his friends who were not saved. I heard the Lord say, "Evil communications corrupt your good manners." (See 1 Corinthians 15:33.) I shared this with my husband, and he said, "I will be OK. I'm not going to drink."

When he came home I noticed he had been drinking. I said to him, "I'm not going through this anymore. I'm done. I'm finished." He asked me to forgive him and kept promising not to drink again. I said, "No, I'm not going to forgive you. I have forgiven you time and time again. No, I'm done." At that same moment when I said, "No, I'm not forgiving you," the Lord spoke to me and said with a very loud, strong voice, "Are you better than me?" I said, "No, Lord, I'm not." He then said, "How dare you deny this man the very thing you are in need of every day of your life!" That's how God wants us to see the act of forgiveness. Since we are always in need of forgiveness, we must always extend forgiveness to others.

Woman of Repentance

> Repent, then, and turn to God, so that your sins may be wiped out, that times of refreshing may come from the Lord.
> —Acts 3:19, niv

Everyone may not have the same struggles in life. We sometimes judge some sins as being greater than others. During the time that I was struggling with my husband's relapse into his old lifestyle, I heard the Lord say, "*All* have sinned and fall short of the glory of God" (Rom. 3:23, niv, emphasis added). I felt the presence of God very strongly. The Holy Spirit convicted me. I wept and repented to the Lord and asked my husband to forgive me for holding unforgiveness, bitterness, and resentment in my heart toward him. I needed to forgive my husband and the women he had been involved with. The Bible says if we do not forgive, neither will our Father in heaven forgive us of our sins. (See Matthew 6:15.)

I was tired of my husband. There were broken promises along with relapses into drinking and drug abuse. I was tired of praying and fasting. After seven years, I was ready to throw in the towel. What I did not understand was that it wasn't that he did not want to stop drinking and doing drugs, but it was an addiction. In fact, it was a generational curse. His dad had an addiction to alcohol and drugs and committed adultery. He followed in line with the curse of addictions and adultery. Then our sons developed the same addictions and also committed adultery. Generational curses go down to the third, fourth, and fifth generations. They are real and need to be broken.

My former pastor has gone on to be with the Lord, but she taught me how to separate the spirit from the person. She would say, "Love the person, but hate the sin."

In some ways, I felt justified in my marriage, because I was not the one drinking, doing drugs, or committing adultery. But I didn't realize that unforgiveness and bitterness are sins, just as hatred, anger, pride and rebellion are. Forgiveness is the key to freedom.

Supernatural encounter

The next day, my husband went to check himself into a rehab. Little did he know God would meet him there. God gave my husband a supernatural, Damascus-Road experience. He told me that while he was on his knees, a bright light came into the room and the Lord said to him, "Don't be afraid. I am with you."

My husband said at that moment he experienced something he had never felt before. He sensed a change in his heart. What was supposed to be a thirty-day program became a one-week stay. Like the story of the prodigal son, he came to himself. God delivered my husband from drinking, drug addiction, and infidelity.

Today, my husband is saved, delivered, and set free by the power of God. He is a man of God and a man of prayer. He covers me, his children, family, friends, and the body of Christ in prayer. My husband is an ordained pastor and teacher. God has used him countless times to help other men receive deliverance from their drinking, drugs, and infidelity. As Luke 22:32 says, "...and when thou art converted, strengthen thy brethren."

Whether it's a troubled marriage or being betrayed, hurt, or molested by family or people in the church, a kingdom woman makes a decision to forgive, it is at that moment the Holy Spirit does a supernatural work to demonstrate forgiveness in our hearts. As I stated earlier, we all have sinned and fallen short of the glory of God. (See Romans 3:23.) We all need God's grace, mercy, and forgiveness.

Woman Overcomer

In Revelation 12:11, it says, "And they overcame him by the blood of the Lamb, and by the word of their testimony; and they loved not their lives unto the death."

Millions of women around the world fight battles no one may know about. But through prayer and persistence, they learn to be overcomers. I share the testimony about my husband not to bring shame or guilt to him but to encourage women who may be in a similar situation to have hope. If God can perform a miracle in my marriage, He can do the same for you. He can restore you and your destiny. What the devil meant for bad, God can turn it for good. All things work together for your good (Rom. 8:28). The process never feels good, but God can make things work together for your good.

Transparency Releases Transformation

The Lord told us to be transparent in our testimony and we would see lives transformed. We have spent many years together praying for broken marriages countless of hours counseling many marriages and families have been healed delivered and restored back to God as a result of our testimony. And to witness this miracle was worth every tear and all the pain I had to endure in my own marriage Glory to God!

God can turn your pain into power, your mess into a message, and give you a miracle marriage.

When God gives you a miracle marriage, there is no residue. When people see us, it appears to them that we have always had such a great life. I have had women say to me, "I envy your life, it seems like you don't have a care in the world," not knowing the years and tears I spent crying to the Lord to bring deliverance and breakthrough in my life and marriage. There is a process that you must go through to become what God has predestined for you to be. Your process may be different, but you too must follow the pathway to purpose.

My Story of Breakthrough and Deliverance

In writing this book, God only allowed me to share just a portion of my life, but truth be told, I've been through much more—through hell and back. If the devil would have had it his way, I would have been dead a long time ago, but because I've been called for such a time as this, and because I have a purpose and destiny the enemy could not destroy me.

It is by God's grace and glory that I don't look like what I've been through. People may see a glimpse of God's glory, but they may not know your whole story. Today, my husband and I consider ourselves like Priscilla and Aquila—an apostolic prophetic team, a dynamic duo.

Kingdom woman, you may have some ups and downs, but don't put on a frown. Wear the crown that fits you. Learn how to smile through your sufferings. "Many are the afflictions of the righteous, but God shall deliver them out of them all" (Ps. 34:19). "Weeping may endure for a night, but joy comes in the morning" (Ps. 30:5). Kingdom woman, if you suffer with Christ, you will reign with Christ. (See 2 Timothy 2:12.)

> Be merciful, just as your Father is merciful.
> —Luke 6:36, niv

I recall another time before we were finally delivered from the trouble in our marriage when it seemed like, the more I prayed, the worse things got. My husband started disc-jockeying on the weekends and wanted me to go with him. For the sake of peace I would go from time to time.

I didn't drink and I didn't do drugs, but my husband

would insist that I order something to drink. So, I would usually order a wine cooler or Pepsi. I often sat there feeling like I didn't belong. I thought, "What if the police come and raid the place?" There was a lot of drug and prostitution trafficking at that club. I thought about the cops coming and taking us all to jail. I was worried about what my church family would say.

I was in the nightclub on Saturday and in church on Sunday. There are some Christians and leaders who live like this now. One night, I sat in the nightclub staring at the Exit sign, wondering what would happen if the nightclub caught on fire and I couldn't get out. I thought I would die in my sins and go to hell, so I went home that night and prayed and asked God to forgive me.

As a result of my decision never to go back into the nightclubs, my husband eventually moved out, leaving me and the children for about two-and-a-half years. It was during this time, while we were separated, that I began to build a deeper relationship with God and received the deliverance that I needed in my own life.

I live today healed, delivered, and restored. I now share this story to give glory to God and to show women like you that God is able. I have borne witness to this truth: that we overcome by the blood of the Lamb and the words of our testimony. (See Revelation 12:11.)

The Bible says God's mercies are new every morning (Lam. 3:23), and as I have said, God saved my husband and called him to be a pastor. God saved the man who was going to kill my husband and called him to be a preacher as well. Wow! Talk about the mercies of God. I could have been a widow and my children could have been fatherless, but God had a purpose for all of our lives. When you hold fast to this truth, you can stand

and endure hardship like a good soldier. As a kingdom woman, you can challenge the enemy and say, "Enough is enough, devil. You can't have my family. You can't have my children, my marriage, my health, my finances, or my destiny. I'm taking them back for the kingdom of God." As the scripture says, "We wrestle not against flesh and blood, but against principalities, against powers, against the rulers of the darkness of this world, against spiritual wickedness in high places" (Eph. 6:12).

The Bible says that some things leave only by prayer and fasting (Mark 9:29). I began to fast twenty-one days at a time. One time I went on a forty-day fast and ended up in the hospital. Nevertheless, because I believed that God had ordained our marriage, I was determined that the devil was not going to win. I made up my mind, he was not going to have my husband. I was determined that my children were not going to grow up without their father. This strategy and result may not apply to every situation. You have to know God's plan for your life.

Although kingdom women sometimes go through hard times, we don't have to stay in abusive relationships when our lives are threatened. However, to those who sense the call to stand in the gap and fight the good fight of faith: don't give up. Ask God to teach your hands how to war and your fingers how to fight. Learn how to separate the spirit from the person. Keep fighting and believe God for the breakthrough.

PART TWO
THE MANTLE

Chapter 5

ANOINTED AND CALLED

The Spirit of the Lord is upon me, because he hath anointed me to preach the gospel to the poor; he hath sent me to heal the brokenhearted, to preach deliverance to the captives, and recovering of sight to the blind, to set at liberty them that are bruised.
—LUKE 4:18

ONE NIGHT I had a dream I was wearing a long white robe and I was standing on top of a mountain, which was more like a big rock. Hundreds of people were at the foot of the mountain, and I was preaching to them from Luke 4:18. The revelation from this verse was coming out of my mouth with great boldness, power, and authority.

When I woke up, I grabbed my Bible to find this scripture. I read it over and over, and began to memorize it. I had all these questions running through my mind: What was that dream all about? Could it be that God was calling me into ministry? I thought to myself, "Surely God must have the wrong person. I don't have that kind of boldness, power, and authority that I had in the dream."

I'm an introvert—quiet, shy, and fearful. At the time, I was too afraid to stand in front of anybody to say anything. When I was in school and the teacher would ask a question, I can recall the many times I knew the answer but would not stand up because I was too afraid. So, having a dream where I was standing before people preaching with great boldness must have been just a dream. Besides, I knew the church I attended was traditional and religious. They did not believe in women preachers.

I kept silent about that dream for years. I was almost ashamed to talk about my encounter, but I secretly continued studying the Word of God. Although my previous pastor would sometimes call me and share things with me, I can't really say she was a mentor. The benefit of having a mentor is that you can learn from all they have learned through trial and error. They can share wisdom with you to help you not make some of the same mistakes they have made.

I believe it is important to have a mentor, just as Elijah mentored Elisha. But what is most important is to have the Holy Spirit teach you and lead you into all truth. (See John 16:13.) Elijah permitted Elisha to accompany him to Gilgal without saying a word about staying someplace, but when he arrived there he told him to stay while he went to Bethel. (See 2 Kings 2:1–6.)

Then Elijah urged him to stay at Bethel while he went to Jericho and to remain at Jericho while he went to Jordan. But Elisha would not leave Elijah. He was determined to go on with him until he was taken to heaven. It could have been that Elijah was testing Elisha to see how determined he was to have his spirit and power. Elisha had already been anointed to take his place, but he had not yet received the spirit and power of Elijah.

In the apostle Paul's letter to the Hebrews, we see that prophets were instructors or mentors in the early church. They instructed the Hebrews in "piety and virtue" and "generally lived retired," being seen in public mainly when they had a message from God to deliver. According to the *Union Bible Dictionary*, "their habitations and mode of life were plain, simple, and consistent. Prophets had pupils who were "trained in religion and habits of devotion."[1]

In the days of Elijah, he was headmaster of several schools in Gilgal and Bethel. Elisha succeeded Elijah over these schools and even enlarged them. Elijah performed sixteen miracles and Elisha thirty-two. You may be called into ministry to do a specific work for God, and although God is ultimately your teacher, sometimes God will send someone to disciple you in your calling. Timothy had Paul, Ruth had Naomi, and Elisha had Elijah.

My introduction to ministry was not as formal as Elisha's introduction. Although I have always desired to have a mentor—someone who would take me under his or her wings to teach and train me in ministry—I did not have the one-on-one training I desired. Yes, God used different people in ministry to teach me from afar, but I lacked the fellowship of consistent mentorship. I suffered in silence in my early years in ministry. I felt inferior to the call of God because of it. I prayed for God to give me a spiritual mom and spiritual dad who would love me. I wanted someone I could talk to and be accountable to. I wanted someone who could teach me and help me grow in ministry. I wanted someone who would give me godly counsel and correction, but for some reason God did not send that kind of person into my life. Nonetheless, I was personally taught by the Lord through the school of the Holy Spirit. The Lord said to me, "I will cause you to become that which you have lacked in your own life." I am grateful that He graced me to be both a natural and spiritual mother even though I had none myself. I still think about mistakes I might not have made if there had been mature mentors to disciple me in ministry.

What Is a Mantle?

A mantle is "a loose, sleeveless cloak or shawl, worn especially by women." It is also "an important role or responsibility that passes from one person to another."[2] Both meanings are used in the story of Elijah and Elisha in 2 King 2:1–15. In this passage we see the role, burden, and duty of a minister represented by the mantle. The prophet Elijah dropped his onto the shoulders of his successor, Elisha, when he passed his ministry on to him.

It is so important to be under a strong, godly covering. By this I mean someone who has been chosen by God, and who is called, anointed, and appointed. This person will cover you, correct you, impart, activate, and stir up the gifts inside of you. The responsibility of stepping into ministry is not something to be taken lightly. There is nothing more precious to God than His people. With that being said, it is not recommended that anyone rush into ministry without understanding the full weight of the role.

Get Ready for the Shift

> Trust in the LORD with all your heart, and lean not on your own understanding; In all your ways acknowledge Him, And He shall direct your paths.
> —Proverbs 3:5–6, NKJV

You may not always see the shift coming, but God will shift you out of one season into the next season. I had been working at a job for eleven years and really loved it. I was making good money. I was able to buy my children clothes from a department store instead of a second-hand store. I had planned to be at that company until the Lord called me home or until the company closed.

At my workstation I had my small pocket Bible. I posted index cards with scriptures to memorize daily. People would often come to me for prayer. It was like a ministry within the workplace.

One day I was singing to the Lord, and in a still, small voice, abruptly interrupted me I heard, "I am going to bring you off this job to preach the gospel." I stopped everything. I stopped singing and stopped my machine. I heard it a second time: "I am going to bring you off this job to preach the gospel." I felt a presence I had never felt before in all my life. I got up and quickly went into a bathroom stall. I fell to my knees and began to cry uncontrollably. Then I heard it a third time: "I am going to bring you off this job to preach the gospel."

People at my job who heard me weeping and crying asked if I was OK. I pulled myself together and went back to work, wondering how this could be. I thought, "There is no way that God could use me to preach the gospel." Besides, I was a woman, and women do not preach—so I thought. That encounter was something I had never experienced before, but I believed it was God speaking to me.

I finally said, "OK, God, I will quit my job, but not right now. I will quit when I save up enough money." When I said that, I felt the presence of the Lord lift off me. The Bible says, "Grieve not the Holy Spirit" (Eph. 4:30). I didn't know at the time that I had grieved the Holy Spirit. I was still a babe in Christ. I continued going to work and hid that experience in my heart for several years. I eventually quit my job and began to trust in the Lord.

So many times we obey God just enough to get what we want. We pray long enough and do all the right things just to get what we want. But obedience is better than sacrifice. (See 1 Samuel 15:22.) Jesus once asked the disciples, "Why do you call Me, 'Lord, Lord,' and not do the things that I say?" (Luke 6:46). When we hear the prompting of the Holy Spirit offering us direction or counsel, we must be quick to respond in obedience, even if the instructions seem intimidating or impossible. Remember, God both calls us and equips us for service. If He is telling you to step out in faith to serve Him in ministry, you must trust that He will be there with you every step of the way.

Chapter 6

A WOMAN OF PRAYER

I exhort therefore, that, first of all, supplications, prayers, intercessions, and giving of thanks, be made for all men; for kings, and for all that are in authority; that we may lead a quiet and peaceable life in all godliness and honesty.
—1 Timothy 2:1–2

As long as I can remember I have always had a passion for prayer. I believe every born-again believer's first call is to establish a relationship with God through prayer. The disciples asked Jesus to teach them how to pray. A kingdom woman also is required to ask the Lord to teach her how to pray.

Prayer should become a lifestyle for the believer. Prayer is a solemn request for help. It is an expression of thanks to God in worship. Spending time in prayer with the Lord is the most important thing. God will train you to hear His voice. Jesus said, "My sheep know my voice, but a stranger they will not follow" (John 10:5, author's paraphrase).

It's through prayer that we will experience God's glory, miracles, signs, and wonders.

A kingdom woman stands at the assigned gate given to her by God. She guards it with governmental prayer. Governmental prayer can be exercised by someone who has been given authority by God to occupy take authority in a particular place or region. Governmental prayers are prayed with authority and power. God has used me to pray and intercede on behalf of my family and for sinners and saints in specific cities and nations. As a result, countless people have received salvation, healing, deliverance, and miracles.

Prayer is a powerful weapon we can use when we pray the Word of God. A prayer mantle is like a prayer shawl. It is like a spiritual shawl upon someone who has been given a special gift to pray and intercede on behalf of others. According to the Word of God we are to "pray without ceasing" because "the effectual fervent prayer of a righteous man availeth much" (1 Thess. 5:17; James 5:16).

Prayer is a privilege. It's a special right or advantage. It is a privilege to communicate with God and to stand in the gap as watchmen and gatekeepers.

Prayer is a priority and not a performance. In Matthew 6:5 Jesus said these words: "And when thou prayest, thou shalt not be as the hypocrites are: for they love to pray standing in the synagogues and in the corners of the streets, that they may be seen of men. Verily I say unto you, They have their reward." Prayer should never be done to be seen of men or to show off. Rather, prayer should be done from a pure heart.

Prayer accesses the power of God. When we pray from a pure heart, our prayers produce power. Zechariah 4:6 says, "Not by might, nor by power, but by [the spirit of the Lord]."

The Bible also says in 1 Timothy 2:1–2, "I exhort therefore, that, first of all, supplications, prayers, intercessions, and giving of thanks, be made for all men; for kings, and for all that are in authority; that we may lead a quiet and peaceable life in all godliness and honesty." God will sometimes give you a word of knowledge or lay people on your heart so you can pray for them. As I began to grow in prayer, God began to reveal things to me. There have been times He has given me dreams about well-known pastors and leaders. Some of them had television programs and had been involved in scandals, abuse, crooked dealings with money in ministry and were committing adultery. Amos 3:7 says these words: "Surely the LORD God will do nothing, but he revealeth his secret unto his servants the prophets." God will reveal His secrets to intercessors He can trust.

A Woman of Holiness

Be ye holy; for I am holy.

—1 Peter 1:16

Follow peace with all men, and holiness, without which no man shall see the Lord.

—Hebrews 12:14

A kingdom woman is a holy woman of God. She emulates the holiness of God. A woman of holiness is not someone who stirs up strife but instead seeks to follow peace, although this can be challenging at times. A woman of holiness has a desire to demonstrate the love of God in order to diffuse or calm a tense situation. A woman of holiness is not one who is haughty, but humble. The Bible says, "Who is like thee, glorious in holiness?" (Exod. 15:11). God is holy, and He is looking for a holy people to serve Him in His kingdom.

What does holiness mean? *Webster's 1828 American Dictionary of the English Language* defines holiness as "the state of being holy; purity or integrity of moral character; freedom from sin; sanctity...Holiness denotes purity or integrity of moral character." Holiness is having a pure heart toward God and others. It is the quality or "state of being holy."[1] It is a life of holiness and total devotion to God. It is having a pure heart toward God and others and being sanctified and set apart for God. Holiness also means having moral goodness and simply treating everyone right in the sight of God.

How do we attain holiness? The Bible says not to be conformed to this world but to be transformed by the renewing of your mind:

> I beseech you therefore, brethren, by the mercies of God, that you present your bodies a living sacrifice, holy, acceptable to God, which is your reasonable service. And do not be conformed to this world, but be transformed by the renewing of your mind, that you may prove what is that good and acceptable and perfect will of God.
> —Romans 12:1–2, NKJV

When God has commanded you to present your body a living sacrifice that means you live a holy life. People should be able to look at your life and know that you are holy. There should be a difference between you and the world. You should not look like the world, dress like the world, or behave like the world.

You don't fornicate and then come to church and sing on the praise and worship team, play the instruments, or serve in leadership positions. When you are called to be a leader, there should be a standard of holiness in your life. Many have lowered the standard of holiness and are compromising. God is restoring holiness back into the church.

Holiness is not a denomination

For years I thought holiness was a denomination, a certain hairstyle, or certain style of dress. I used to work with two women who confessed holiness. They wore their hair pulled back in a bun and wore long skirts and dresses. They went to a Holiness church but did not demonstrate the characteristic of true holiness. I watched them come to work late, gossip and talk about other people, and look down on other women who wore pants and make-up. I was discouraged to see these two women confess holiness but not display the character of holiness.

I wore pants to work, but they were never mean toward me. They were always inviting me to come to church with them. I thought, "If this is holiness or if this is how church people act, I don't want any part of it." One Friday when we got off work they told me that their church was having a revival and asked if I would come. During that time I was still struggling in my marriage, and I knew my husband would be gone the entire weekend at the nightclub, so I decided to go to church with them. I hoped that by going to church with them the pain in my heart would stop.

I had a great time and was glad I went. We danced and shouted most of the night. When we came to work on Monday word began to spread that I went to church with the Holiness women. Other coworkers began to make fun of me. They made comments about how I couldn't wear pants anymore.

I got upset and said, "Just because I went to church with them doesn't mean I have to stop wearing pants." Then I firmly stated, "I am not taking my pants off for anyone, not even God."

Apparently I did not realize what I had said. All day while I was at work that statement kept ringing in my ears as a question: "Not even God?" As I was driving home I heard a still, small voice say, "When you get home take everything out of your closet that you do not need and put it in bags." There were certain clothes I wore to the nightclub with my husband. The majority of them were pants. After cleaning my closet out, basically all I had were a few skirts and dresses.

When I was finished, a peace came over me, although I had gotten rid of my pants. I began to think about what I had confessed. The statement that I made—"I am not taking my pants off for anyone, not even God"—made me wonder if pants had become an idol in my life. Idolatry is an excessive devotion to or worship of a person or thing, and I had an extreme love for wearing pants. As I prayed about it, I realized that some memories from my childhood were heavy on my mind and connected to this issue. I thought if a girl had on a dress it was an easier way for the molester to abuse her. Could that mean I didn't trust God to protect me? God used these two women of holiness to help break me free from the bondage of fear that I had been dealing with since childhood, a bondage that had manifested itself in the form of my own idolatry of pants. That certainly doesn't mean pants are bad for all women to wear, but in that season of my life God needed me to demonstrate that

I was willing to trust Him to protect me more than I trusted wearing pants.

The church I eventually joined did not believe in women wearing pants. They used Deuteronomy 22:5—"The woman shall not wear that which pertaineth unto a man"—to support their teaching against women in pants. I complied with the rules of that church for thirteen years, but since then God has given me revelation of that scripture. When I go shopping I do not go into the men's department to shop; I shop in the women's department and therefore am not in violation of that scripture.

I'm making this point because some people are looked down upon if they do not wear dresses. This is still an issue in many different denominations. There are some churches that will not allow a woman to preach in their church with pants, makeup, or jewelry on. I'm not here to argue the point whether or not a woman can wear pants but on a personal standpoint I believe that God doesn't care if women wear pants or dresses. The Bible says, "Man looks at the outward appearance, but the Lord looks at the heart" (1 Sam. 16:7, NKJV). I believe that long as our clothes are not too tight, not too revealing, or too short we are OK. The Lord is pleased when we dress in modesty and holiness. We must continue to pray for freedom and liberty, because "where the Spirit of the Lord is, there is liberty" (2 Cor. 3:17).

Who Is This Kingdom Woman?

> I will praise thee; for I am fearfully and wonderfully made: marvellous are thy works; and that my soul knoweth right well. My substance was not

> hid from thee, when I was made in secret, and curiously wrought in the lowest parts of the earth. Thine eyes did see my substance, yet being unperfect; and in thy book all my members were written, which in continuance were fashioned, when as yet there was none of them. How precious also are thy thoughts unto me, O God! how great is the sum of them! If I should count them, they are more in number than the sand: when I awake, I am still with thee.
>
> —Psalm 139:14–18

Do you know who you are? You may have asked the Lord countless times, "Who am I?" In order for you to know who you are you must go to the One who created you. It's in Him that you discover who you are and why you have been created. Psalm 139 gives a short description of who you are. A kingdom woman is one who praises and worships the King. She fears and reverences Him. She knows that she was wonderfully made. She knows that she is a work of her Creator. He has fashioned her right. She knows that God put substance, value, and worth inside of her. She understands that even though she's imperfect, everything about her—good or bad—has already been written in God's Word. She takes comfort in knowing that God knows all about her, yet His thoughts are precious toward her. She's assured that all the days of her life, the Lord will be with her.

A kingdom woman is the daughter of the sovereign King. She is crowned with character and clothed with confidence. This kingdom woman is made in the image and the likeness of God, as it says in Genesis 1:26: "And God said, 'Let us make man in our image, after our likeness: and let them have dominion.'" I encourage you to walk in the power and authority given to you by God. Govern the gates and rule with the scepter of righteousness and holiness.

A kingdom woman is a worshiper of God. She's a worshiping warrior. She has learned how to praise God in the midst of her circumstances, like David, who wrote, "I will bless the LORD at all times. My soul shall make her boast in the LORD: the humble shall hear thereof, and be glad" (Ps. 34:1–2). She makes a decision to bless God at all times, and His praise shall continually be in her mouth. A kingdom woman will not allow her situations, background, or past failures to determine who she will become.

Worthy of His Glory

> Who shall ascend into the hill of the LORD? or who shall stand in his holy place? He that hath clean hands, and a pure heart; who hath not lifted up his soul unto vanity, nor sworn deceitfully. He shall receive the blessing from the LORD, and righteousness from the God of his salvation. This is the generation of them that seek him, that seek thy face, O Jacob. Selah. Lift up your heads, O ye gates; and be ye lift up, ye everlasting doors; and the King of glory shall come in. Who is this King of glory? The LORD strong and mighty, the LORD mighty in battle. Lift up your heads, O ye gates; even lift them up, ye everlasting doors; and the King of glory shall come in. Who is this King of glory? The LORD of hosts, he is the King of glory. Selah.
>
> —PSALM 24:3–10

When we allow the King of glory to come into our lives, He comes in strong and mighty. The scriptures tell us He is "mighty in battle" (Ps. 24:8). He is our battle-axe in warfare. When you experience His glory, you experience God! When we allow the King of glory to come, He will break open generational gates that have been closed. With His glory comes divine deliverance, healing, breakthroughs, miracles, signs, and wonders. When the glory comes upon your life, darkness turns to light. You can walk in and change the atmosphere of neighborhoods, cities, countries, and nations.

You are worthy of carrying His glory. When kingdom women develop a lifestyle of worship, prayer, holiness, and deliverance, and spend time studying God's Word, they become glory carriers. A glory carrier is a person who carries the glory of God. Glory carriers are people who ascend to high places. They ascend to heavenly places. Glory carriers carry the oil of God on their life. You can tell those who spend time in God's presence; they are "oily." Glory rests upon their countenance. They walk with a special distinction. They stand in His holy place with clean hands and a pure heart. Glory carriers are blessed and righteous. They are God-seekers. They are revealers of the King. They point people to the King.

I have experienced God's glory in my life. I was blind, but now I see. I was sick, but now I'm healed. I was bound, but now I'm free. Kingdom woman, as you make prayer and holiness priorities in your life, you too will become a carrier of the glory of God.

Chapter 7

AUTHORITY, POWER, AND DEMONSTRATION

I will give unto thee the keys of the kingdom of heaven.
—MATTHEW 16:19

K EYS REPRESENT AUTHORITY. Do you remember when you received your first keys to your car or home? It's a feeling you can't quite explain. I'm sure you felt good knowing that you were given keys to access something that belonged to you. A kingdom woman has access to heaven through kingdom prayers.

God has given you keys of the kingdom to unlock strategies against Satan's kingdom and against principalities, to break curses of sickness, and to break curses of poverty. God has put keys of prosperity into your hands to unlock blessings that have been held back for years. God says, "I will use women to change cultures, cities, communities, and nations for revival. Yes, even the White House. I shall unlock justice, for when the righteous are in authority the people rejoice; when the wicked are in authority the people mourn."

God is raising up women who will be problem solvers, women with solutions in our society. No longer will women be afraid to say what they are seeing or be afraid to go and do what God is leading them to do. God told me this about the women He is preparing and to whom He is giving the keys to the future:

> *I will give you the keys to unlock and take the muzzle off the mouth of other women who have suffered in silence for years. They will speak to the old systems, to the old waste place that has caused many to die spiritually. They will speak and say, "You shall not die but live and declare the works of the Lord."*
>
> *I will send you to those who have been broken and bound by chains and fetters. I'm sending you to unlock the prison doors.*
>
> *Know that I have given you keys of the kingdom to unlock doors of opportunity; keys to unlock breakthroughs; keys to unlock wisdom and wealth; keys to unlock business, destiny, and dreams; and keys to unlock salvation, healing, and restoration.*
>
> *These are days that I am birthing an apostolic age. I'm releasing angelic angels that are ascending and descending even now to assist you in your assignment and in your mandate.*
>
> *I give you keys to advance My kingdom, to release My glory from generation to generation, that you may leave a legacy to legislate justice in the earth. And you shall experience My favor—fresh fire falling upon you—for My kingdom is within you, and you will see*

miracles, signs, and wonders. But seek ye first the kingdom of God, and all these things shall be added unto you, says the Lord.

Twelve Kingdom Keys

Kingdom keys help us to spiritually unlock what God has ordained to be unlocked in our lives. They also help us lock out whatever God has not ordained for our lives. These keys have been given to every believer, but it's up to us to learn how to appropriate these keys.

1. Key of prayer—"Pray without ceasing" (1 Thess. 5:16).
2. Key of worship—"Worship him in spirit and truth" (John 4:24).
3. Key of salvation—"Thou art the God of my salvation" (Ps. 25:5).
4. Key of deliverance—"But upon mount Zion shall be deliverance" (Obad. 1:17).
5. Key of miracles—"After that miracles, then gifts of healings" (1 Cor. 12:28).
6. Key of glory—"The glory of the Lord is risen upon thee" (Isa. 60:1).
7. Key of authority—"When the righteous are in authority…" (Prov. 29:2).
8. Key of knowledge—"And my lips shall utter knowledge" (Job 33:3).
9. Key of power—"Behold I give unto you power" (Luke 10:19).

10. Key of wisdom—"Wisdom is the principal thing" (Prov. 4:7).

11. Key of favor—"So shalt thou find favor" (Prov. 3:4).

12. Key of wealth—"For it is he that giveth thee power to get wealth" (Deut. 8:18).

Father, we thank You for kingdom keys to exercise our authority as believers to process our inheritance.

Woman Commander

Hast thou commanded the morning since thy days; and caused the dayspring to know his place; that it might take hold of the ends of the earth, that the wicked might be shaken out of it?
—Job 38:12–13

As a spiritual soldier it is our duty to command the morning and decree and declare that wickedness be shaken out of the earth, our lives, our homes, and our families. Every morning after my husband would leave go to work, I would spend hours commanding the morning through prayer, memorizing scriptures, and making decrees on behalf of my family, friends, and others.

Thou shalt decree a thing, and it shall be established unto thee and the light shall shine upon thy ways.
—Job 22:28

Here is a prayer I used to pray for my husband:

I decree and declare that the devil will not hold my husband as a prisoner against his will. I decree and declare that all addictions—smoking, drinking, drugs, and adultery—will no longer be a part of my husband's life. I take authority over demon spirits holding him as a prisoner against his will, and I bind you in the name of Jesus. Devil, you are a liar. I cancel every diabolical plot, plan, scheme, and every wicked device against his life. I bind every bloodline curse and every generational curse of drugs, drinking, addiction, and adultery. I evict you and eradicate you. I command you to leave. Get out of his life, never to return again.

I bind generational curses that have come down through the bloodline: curses of addictions, curses of abandonment, curses of drugs, curses of drinking, and curses of adultery.

I decree and declare that my husband will have a supernatural encounter, a Damascus-Road experience. Lord, Your Word declares whatsoever I bind on Earth shall be bound in heaven. I thank You for delivering him from bloodline and generational curses. Thank You that he is set free. Thank You, Lord, my husband is saved. Thank You, Lord, that my husband is a man of God, a man of prayer, and a man of wisdom. I thank You that he is a man who studies the Word of God. Lord, I thank You that he will preach and teach the gospel.

Lord, Your Word declares that "whosoever believeth in [Me] should not perish, but have

> *everlasting life" (John 3:16). I decree my husband shall not perish but shall have everlasting life. Lord, Your Word declares that if I got saved you would save my house. "The unbelieving husband is sanctified by the wife" (1 Cor. 7:14). Lord, I thank You that You are able to save to the uttermost. Thank You, Lord.*
>
> *Whatsoever I loose on Earth shall be loosed in heaven. I begin to loose new mercy, new grace, new salvation, new deliverance, new healing, new miracles, signs, and wonders.*

Use your authority to command and decree

What was I doing with these prayers? I was calling "those things which be not as though they were" (Rom. 4:17). I had been faithfully praying, even though my husband wasn't walking in any of the things I prayed for. The Bible says "we walk by faith, not by sight" (2 Cor. 5:7). I kept loving him. I kept praying and fasting. I kept making decrees over his life. I continued standing in the gap on his behalf. I was praying and decreeing continually. The Bible says, "What things soever ye desire, when ye pray, believe that ye receive them, and ye shall have them" (Mark 11:24). Don't underestimate the power of prayer.

It was through a painful marriage that God began to teach me how to pray. Pain has a way of pushing you into the presence of God. I began to do word studies on prayer. I memorized scriptures on prayer. For example, these are some verses I memorized and still pray on behalf of those who need salvation:

- Psalm 55:17—Morning, noon, and midnight, I will pray it!
- Job 22:28—I will decree it!
- Job 38:12—I will command it!
- Ezekiel 37:4—I will prophesy it!
- Ps. 34:1—I will put praise on it!

A Woman General

A woman general is the commander of an army. She sees her family as her army, and as an intercessor she stands in the gap on their behalf. She seeks God for strategies that will put an end to generational curses that have been passed down from one generation to the next. A woman general knows her rank, draws a line in the sand, and decrees, "The curse stops here!"

Women commanders are called to legislate in the earth. *To legislate* means "to make or enact laws."[1] As a kingdom woman, you have a scepter of righteousness to make laws and to release justice against injustice in the earth. You have a charge to prophetically discern the call of God on your life and then, through the Holy Spirit, to help point others in the direction of their destiny.

Romans 8:19 tells us "the creation waits with eager longing for the revealing of the sons [and daughters] of God" (NIV). God is calling apostolic women to release uncompromised, undiluted decrees into the atmosphere. Kingdom woman, no matter what your circumstances look like in the natural, if God has given you a promise, stand on the Word of God and fight until you win. You may not see any results right away, but continue to pray until God releases you.

> Wherefore he is able also to save them to the uttermost that come unto God by him, seeing he ever liveth to make intercession for them.
> —Hebrews 7:25

A Woman of Power

> Behold, I give unto you power to tread upon serpents and scorpions, and over all the power of the enemy: and nothing shall by any means hurt you.
> —Luke 10:19

One Saturday morning years ago, before I matured in my understanding of God's call on the lives of kingdom women, I had the Gospel radio station on while I was cleaning my house. It was a woman pastor preaching on deliverance. She spoke with such power and authority. She was commanding demon spirits of fear, rejection, deep hurts, broken-heartedness, a wounded spirit, addictions, lust, perversion, and marriage-breaking spirits to leave! I had never heard anything like that before in my life.

After losing my mom to cancer, I backslid, but I had recently rededicated my life back to God. I spoke in tongues and knew I loved God, but I kept feeling like something was missing. I felt like there had to be something more. Growing up, I had gone through so much pain. I never dealt with my inner issues. Listening to this woman pastor who was anointed in deliverance, I realized that deliverance was the thing that was missing in my life. Even though I didn't understand deliverance at that time, my spirit connected to what she was saying.

At the end of the broadcast, she gave the address of her church. I was so excited that I wrote down the information to the church and made a decision to go not long after. When that Sunday morning came I got up early with my four children to drive an hour and a half to go to that church.

Our family used to belong to a Pentecostal church when I was younger, so I felt right at home, but I had never been to a church like that as an adult. After the pastor finished preaching, she began to minister deliverance. I had never seen anyone with that kind of boldness, power, and authority. As she began to command demon spirits to leave, many people were screaming, coughing, hacking, and crying.

It was a deliverance church, and I knew in my spirit that was the kind of ministry God had ordained for me. I sat there thinking to myself, "One day God is going to use me cast demons out of people and help people get set free." I felt like this was exactly what I was supposed to do—preach deliverance and cast out demons. I knew in my spirit that I was called to this type of ministry. I wanted to know how to help people get set free because I knew the pain of being in prison.

As the service continued, I was fascinated with several things about this woman preacher. She was a woman pastoring a church. She was anointed to preach the gospel. She was not afraid to cast out demons. She demonstrated great power and authority and was a confident woman.

There are so many seeking titles and position and very few seeking deliverance from demons. However, I knew I needed more deliverance. I needed to be set free. I went down for ministry, and I got a lot of deliverance that day. Afterward I felt so clean and free. God was taking me through the process of deliverance and helping me demonstrate the power of a confident woman.

Every week I asked my husband to go with me. Yet, each week he would always say, "You don't have to drive that far to go to church." The drive was not a problem for me, because I was very familiar with Chicago and because I was desperate to be delivered. It didn't matter how far I had to drive to get the help I needed. You might say I was hungry for deliverance. The Bible says, "Those who hunger and thirst for righteousness...shall be satisfied" (Matt. 5:6, ESV). After all, deliverance is "the children's bread" (Matt. 15:26).

I wanted to learn more about deliverance. I bought every book I could buy on deliverance. Every morning I would get up at 5:00 a.m. to listen to deliverance pastors on the radio. I also watched deliverance services on television. I saw and heard pastors on television command demons to leave and teach on taking authority over demon spirits.

I began to seek out other deliverance ministries in my area. In the eighties, I knew of three strong local deliverance ministries, and I started going to deliverance services at these churches three times a week. The Lord taught me so much through these ministries. Two of the pastors have gone on to be with the Lord, and the third one is Apostle John Eckhardt. He has written several books on deliverance.

I was learning so much, and it was so exciting to me. God was training me in the deliverance ministry, and years later I began ministering deliverance to others.

Setting the Captives Free

There are people who are in desperate need of deliverance. A kingdom woman not only walks in personal deliverance but also helps others to walk in it as well. Will you answer the call to be a deliverer? Deliverance is a part of becoming a kingdom woman. The enemy of our souls uses generational curses or assigns areas of temptation to our lives at birth to try to cause us to stumble. God will anoint you with power to help others who are bound and break the chains of bondages off their lives. I pray you will choose to be a deliverer and set the captives free in Jesus's name.

> [For I am] confident of this, that he who began a good work in you will carry it on to completion until the day of Christ Jesus.
> —Philippians 1:6, NIV

God is raising up women who will demonstrate miracles of God—confident women who are positive, self-assured, and level-headed. These kingdom women are firmly trusting, bold, and spiritually equipped for service. To be a confident kingdom woman who walks in power and authority to help set the captives free, you need the spirit of the Lord to be upon your life.

The work that God assigns to us will be perfected until we are no longer able to fulfill that work or we transition to heaven. It is our job as kingdom women to walk confidently in that calling all the days of our life because He who called us is faithful to equip us for that vocation. When we trust Him and step out in faith, lives will be transformed.

PART THREE
THE MINISTRY

Chapter 8

WHAT DOES THE BIBLE SAY ABOUT WOMEN IN MINISTRY AND LEADERSHIP?

There is neither male nor female; for you are all one in Christ Jesus.
—GALATIANS 3:28, NKJV

DO WOMEN HAVE a place in ministry? If so, to what extent does Scripture teach on women having a position of authority in the church? What does the Bible really say about this issue? To understand God's intentions, we must go back to the very beginning. This will help us to see His original purpose for both men and woman.

MALE AND FEMALE CREATED HE THEM

> So God created man in his own image, in the image of God created he him; male and female created he them.
> —GENESIS 1:27

> Male and female created he them; and blessed them, and called their name Adam, in the day when they were created.
> —Genesis 5:2

Adam and Eve were created with distinctive and unique qualities. Their differences were not a source of discord or inequality but a beautiful complement to each other. "Together, God gave them the task of overseeing and ruling His creation."[1] The same relationship is true in ministry today.

Perhaps you are thinking that, although we have laid a biblical foundation for there being neither male nor female in Christ, certain verses in the New Testament still seem to ban women from ministry positions in the church. Part of the reason for that thought is that some of the traditionally minded church members and leaders continue to struggle with the thought of women in ministry or women being in the pulpit. Often scriptures like these are cited as evidence against allowing women in ministry or women into the pulpit:

> Let your women keep silence in the churches: for it is not permitted unto them to speak; but they are commanded to be under obedience as also saith the law.
> —1 Corinthians 14:34

> Let the woman learn in silence with all subjection. But I suffer not a woman to teach, nor to usurp authority over the man, but to be in silence.
> —1 Timothy 2:11–12

These verses are two of many that have been misinterpreted. "In these verses Paul cannot be addressing the women who were already in ministry but rather those in the congregation who were out of order. We have many proofs, many from Paul himself, of women who were all in influential positions of leadership in the early church."[2] We will discuss this later.

"When we understand more about how they used to worship during the time this message was written to the Corinthian church, it helps us to better understand how little the literal meaning applies to our contemporary church. The notes for 1 Corinthians 14:34 in the *Dake Annotated Reference Bible*, give historical information to help us understand the practical context of this Scripture."[3]

> It was a Jewish custom for men to be on one side and the women to be on the other side of the synagogue. (Now, in the twenty-first century, this is still being practiced in some traditional denominational churches.) When men and women were not allowed to sit together it made it difficult for the women to hear the teachings, given where the teacher was standing. The women would speak out because they could not hear or had questions and concerns, and it was at that time the women were instructed to keep silent in the church. He instructed the women if they had any questions to let them ask their husbands at home to keep from disrupting him while teaching. Paul was addressing a specific problem in this scripture instead of issuing a proclamation about women in leadership. This would work in their society and in the context of their church, but with today's churches having more women members than men and with many of those women being unmarried

instead of married, we see that the message needs to be understood in context.

Another source of confusion on the topic of women in ministry relates to the matter of headship over women. The issue is not if a woman can do the job. The Bible does not say women cannot serve. There is no command from God that women cannot be in leadership of the church. The real issue is whether or not she can have authority over males as members of the congregation, as well as females and children. This is the issue we duck, dodge, and dance around. The following passage is usually a basis for this idea:

> Wives, submit yourselves unto your own husbands, as unto the Lord. For the husband is the head of the wife, even as Christ is the head of the church: and he is the saviour of the body.
> —EPHESIANS 5:22–23

Read carefully: "Wives, submit yourselves unto your own husbands, as unto the Lord." For some reason many people think this scripture is proof that women cannot be in leadership positions over men. However, when we read that scripture closely we see that men are not the head of all women. A man is head of his own wife, not the head of every wife or every woman. There is no automatic superiority given to males over all women, and the headship of a male to his own wife does not transfer to the church. No bishop, apostle, or pastor is the head of the Lord's church. Christ is the head of His own church. We all serve at His pleasure. We are His Bride. We all are called to submit to our Head, the Lord Jesus Christ.

Having a woman in a church leadership position does not create any conflict with this order.

As we can see from a closer look at these two scriptures, a better understanding of context and the message's purpose shows that there is nothing wrong with having women in leadership positions.

Understanding Biblical Submission

> "If you are willing and obedient, you shall eat the good of the land; but if you resist and rebel, you will be devoured by the sword." For the mouth of the LORD hath spoken it.
> —Isaiah 1:19–20, NIV

From the beginning of time, Satan has tried to deceive mankind to get him submit to him and not God. As a believer, our heart's desire should be to submit to God. I believe this is one area in which the devil attacks us the most: submitting to God, submitting to His Word, and His will. The Bible says, "Submit yourselves therefore to God. Resist the devil, and he will flee from you" (James 4:7).

In most relationships, submission is often misunderstood. The Bible says to submit "one to another in the fear of God" (Eph. 5:21). Truthfully, submission was not meant to give people permission to dominate or have control over another human being. Submission is respecting someone else's opinion, whether you agree or disagree. *Submission* is not a bad word. Submission is a sign of humbling yourself and surrendering your will to God's Word. Even Christ submitted Himself to the Father, as when He said, "Not my will, but thine, be done" (Luke 22:42).

Some women may have a problem with submitting to their husband, especially if he is not a Christian. But a woman of wisdom treats her husband like a king. Even if he does not act like a king, make him feel like a king. Abigail walked in wisdom with her husband even when he did not make the right decision.

I believe one of the biggest mistakes that some women make is that they sometimes show more respect to their pastors than they do their own husband. This brings hostility toward pastors, and husbands often do not want to attend church because of it. Some women serve and cook for the church more than they do at home. Let me share some wisdom with you: Your husband may not be on the spiritual level you desire him to be, but he is still your husband, and he is your head. He is the one who is supposed to cover and protect you. Respect him like a king, and maybe, just maybe, he will start acting like a king.

Kingdom woman, you must understand that you have a responsibility to submit to God and His Word. Remember, wisdom is, "Submitting yourselves one to another in the fear of God" (Eph. 5:21). Walking in this wisdom is a part of submission. The Bible says, "Wisdom is the principal thing; therefore get wisdom: and with all thy getting get understanding" (Prov. 4:7–9). You are called to submit to wisdom, not foolishness. For example, if your spouse mismanages money, doesn't pay your mortgage, overdrafts your account, and withholds money from you for household expenses, it is not wise to submit to that use of finances. In my case, my husband used money to support his drinking and drug habit, so I did not submit to him handling the money.

Sometimes we use the word *submit* out of its context.

You must learn to submit to God's Word, which is wisdom, not foolishness. When a kingdom woman submits to the King of kings, He will deal with her husband. When we get the revelation from the Holy Spirit concerning this headship, we all will see one another in the light of God's Word and serve with equality.

THE ABIGAIL ANOINTING: A LESSON IN WISE SUBMISSION

Abigail is one of the Bible's great peacemakers. We see in 1 Samuel 25 that she was generous, quick-witted, and wise. Her name means "my father is joy,"[4] and God used her to save lives.

There was a time in my life I felt like I could relate to Abigail, because my husband did not understand certain things in my ministry; he fought against them. He was like the apostle Paul, who before his conversion (when he was still called Saul) was killing Christians and thought he was doing the right thing. It wasn't until he had a Damascus Road experience that he changed. Now, my husband is my number one supporter and fan in ministry.

Abigail has a lot to teach us about wise, biblical submission. Below are just some of the qualities she demonstrates in 1 Samuel 25, qualities that all wives can learn from regardless of their husband's actions.

1. [Abigail] was a woman of good understanding (clever and wise) (verse 3).

2. She was beautiful but not proud or self-exalted (verse 3).

3. She was humble and godly—unspoiled regardless of her riches (verses 2, 6, and 23–35).

4. She had a sense of appreciation for anything others did to aid her household in any degree (verses 14–19).

5. She was reasonable, listened to her servants and sought to protect her unworthy husband as well as all her household from danger (verses 14–35).

6. She was quick to act in time of danger to protect her own (verses 17–19).

7. She did not nag at her husband for his mean and rude character and temper, but patiently lived with him, tolerating the abuse which she no doubt received from such a man (verses 3, 19, 36).

8. She was generous of spirit, seeking to help meet the needs of others (verse 18).

9. She was independent enough to act without the consent of her husband when it was to his good and the good of others concerned (verses 19, 36).

10. She was bold and businesslike in meeting the problems of life; she did not become panic-stricken (verses 17–35).

11. She was brave and willing to face danger, which might involve her own life and certainly that of others. Alone, she faced an

entire army that was coming to destroy her household (verses 19–35).

12. She was gracious and pliable when it was necessary (verses 23–35).

13. She was willing to take blame and be personally responsible for the acts and sins of another whom she sought to reconcile to the one offended (verses 24, 25, 28).

14. She was courteous in her dealings with an enemy and one who had already passed the death sentence on all men of her household (verses 23–35).

15. She had wisdom enough to recognize the kind of temper her husband had and put him in the proper class, while, at the same time, she loved him and tried to save him from harm (verse 25).

16. She was diplomatic in her approach and appeal to the enemy of her household, turning his wrath to mercy and leniency (verses 26–35).

17. She had faith in God and recognized His plan in Israel concerning the one who sought to do her harm (verses 28–35).

18. She was zealous to keep even an enemy spotless in life and conduct (verses 28–31).

19. She wisely kept from her husband the report of the great danger he had been in until he was sober and sensible enough to discuss it (verses 36–38).

20. She was willing to forgive the wrongs intended against her and her house, and soon afterward accepted the very man as a husband who was responsible for these evil plans of evil (verses 39–42).[5]

COMPETITION AMONG WOMEN

The apostle Paul had women who were in leadership positions with him in ministry. He saw how the women needed to iron out their differences. Virtuous kingdom women encourage, equip, and empower each other.

Euodia and Syntyche

When Paul saw that these women had strife and issues among themselves, he pleaded with them to stop quarreling and be friends. God doesn't want His children holding grudges or being at war with one another.

> I urge Euodia and Syntyche to iron out their differences and make up. God doesn't want his children holding grudges. And, oh, yes, Syzygus, since you're right there to help them work things out, do your best with them. These women worked for the Message hand in hand with Clement and me, and with the other veterans—worked as hard as any of us. Remember, their names are also in the Book of Life. Celebrate God all day, every day. I mean, revel in him! Make it as clear as you can to all you meet that you're on their side, working with them and not against them. Help them see that the Master is about to arrive. He could show up any minute! Don't fret or worry. Instead of worrying, pray. Let petitions and praises shape

your worries into prayers, letting God know your concerns. Before you know it, a sense of God's wholeness, everything coming together for good, will come and settle you down. It's wonderful what happens when Christ displaces worry at the center of your life. Summing it all up, friends, I'd say you'll do best by filling your minds and meditating on things true, noble, reputable, authentic, compelling, gracious—the best, not the worst; the beautiful, not the ugly; things to praise, not things to curse. Put into practice what you learned from me, what you heard and saw and realized. Do that, and God, who makes everything work together, will work you into his most excellent harmonies.
—PHILIPPIANS 4:2–9, THE MESSAGE

I urge Euodia and I urge Syntyche to agree and to work in harmony in the Lord. Indeed, I ask you too, my true companion, to help these women [to keep on cooperating], for they have shared my struggle in the [cause of the] gospel, together with Clement and the rest of my fellow workers, whose names are in the Book of Life.
—PHILIPPIANS 4:2–3, AMP

Now I appeal to Euodia and Syntyche. Please, because you belong to the Lord, settle your disagreement. And I ask you, my true partner, to help these two women, for they worked hard with me in telling others the Good News. They worked along with Clement and the rest of my co-workers, whose names are written in the Book of Life.
—PHILIPPIANS 4:2–3, NLT

And now I want to plead with those two dear women, Euodias and Syntyche. Please, please, with

> the Lord's help, quarrel no more—be friends again. And I ask you, my true teammate, to help these women, for they worked side by side with me in telling the Good News to others; and they worked with Clement, too, and the rest of my fellow workers whose names are written in the Book of Life.
>
> —PHILIPPIANS 4:2–3, TLB

The Expositor's Bible Commentary explains:

> The apostle turns from his general exhortation to encouraging them to apply what they have learned. Two women, Euodia and Syntyche, are instructed to bring their attitudes into harmony. Paul does not indicate which one was wrong but for them to get along.[6]

The *Asbury Bible Commentary* also notes that the need for unity and collaboration comes to the surface. Euodia and Syntyche were no doubt influential leaders. Paul stresses the need for mutual cooperation toward reconciliation and unity. Disunity in the church should not be tolerated.[7]

> I beseech Euodias, and beseech Syntyche, that they be of the same mind in the Lord. And I intreat thee also, true yokefellow, help those women which laboured with me in the gospel, with Clement also, and with other my fellow labourers, whose names are in the book of life.
>
> —PHILIPPIANS 4:2–3

Rachel and Leah

> And when Rachel saw that she bare Jacob no children, Rachel envied her sister; and said unto Jacob, Give me children, or else I die. And Jacob's anger was kindled against Rachel: and he said, Am I in God's stead, who hath withheld from thee the fruit of the womb?...And Rachel said, With great wrestlings have I wrestled with my sister, and I have prevailed.
> —GENESIS 30:1–2, 8

Notice what happened when Rachel "saw." The scripture says, "Rachel saw that she bare Jacob no children" (v. 1). You see, that was her first mistake—watching what her sister was doing. As long as you are focused on what others are doing, you can miss what God is saying to you.

The next thing we see is that Rachel "envied her sister" (v. 1). Envy is grieving at the good of another. As long as you envy your sister, you cannot be elevated. When you cannot celebrate your sister's success, chances are you have not developed a level of maturity. God will withhold your blessings until you get your heart right and until He knows He can trust you to handle the level of responsibility.

Last, "Rachel...said unto Jacob, Give me children, or else I die" (v. 1). Rachel was looking to have a child in order to be content. She wanted what Leah had. Coveting and competition has crept into the church. These things must be confronted, not covered up. There's no room for cover girls when it comes to sin. Let us carefully watch against all the risings and workings of poison in our lives.

Remember these lessons from Rachel's story:

1. A child (or any other thing) will not bring you satisfaction or contentment.
2. God warns us of idolatry (putting other things before Him).
3. We are to seek God first before going to anyone else.

Rachel Versus Hannah

Let's take a look at the differences between Rachel and Hannah.

> Rachel envied, but Hannah wept. Rachel...[was desperate for] children, and she died...[while having her] second. Hannah prayed for...[one] child, and she had four more. Rachel is importunate and peremptory, Hannah is submissive and devout. [Hannah said,] "If thou wilt give me a child, I will give him to the Lord [1 Sam.1:11]. Rachel resented Leah. Hannah resented no one. Let Hannah be imitated, and not Rachel, and let our desires be always under the conduct and check of reason and religion.[8]

In the church today, some Christians are in competition for who has the biggest church and who has the most members. Some Christians are also stuck on who has the most luxurious house, car, etc. They think by having all these things, they will be content. This is what Rachel thought too. But God is raising up virtuous, kingdom women who will connect with each other, celebrate each other's victories, and collaborate for the good of all women. God is raising up a company of women who will not be in competition with one another but will stand together to cancel the plans of the enemy and see change come to the church. We are all pressing toward the prize of the high calling of God. Kingdom women want to see everyone win, not just themselves.

An Outpouring of Christ Culture

There is an outpouring of Christ culture coming to the earth. God is not prejudiced. He does not look at gender or color. God pours out His Spirit upon all flesh, male and female. Kingdom women are coming from outside of the walls of the church to reach and teach other women of all backgrounds: black, white, Hispanic, Asian, and everyone in between.

You are called to connect with women with the same apostolic DNA from around the world for global glory gatherings. You are to collaborate with the next generation as well. God wants us to connect the way Mary connected with Elizabeth, and Ruth connected with Naomi.

We live in a unique time in history, and God has placed each one of us in a unique position. The opportunities for Christian women today are immense, and it's time for women to arise. Whether you are young or old, whatever your racial heritage, whatever your upbringing or background, whatever your ability, whatever your present circumstances—the Lord wants to raise you up, equip you, and release you to advance His kingdom. God does not always choose the most likely or the most talented to bring blessing to the body of Christ. He will choose those who are willing and yielded to Him.

The purpose of God pouring out His Spirit is for you to have life more abundantly. God wants you to live a life of purity, power, prosperity, and productivity. God will not pour new wine into old wineskins of tradition and religion. God is pouring out new oil for kingdom women to pray, preach, prophesy, lay hands on the sick, cast out devils, teach, train, and activate others. As the Word says, "Freely you have received; [now] freely give [to others]" (Matt. 10:8, NIV).

Chapter 9

THE KINGDOM WOMAN AND DIVINE ALLIANCES

Admonish the young women to love their husbands, to love their children, to be discreet, chaste, homemakers, good, obedient to their own husbands, that the word of God may not be blasphemed.
—TITUS 2:4–5, NKJV

A KINGDOM WOMAN'S FIRST ministry is to the Lord. Her second ministry is to her family. She should place most of her effort toward helping her family align with God's purpose.

When I became a stay-at-home mom I frequently got up at five o'clock in the morning to pray, worship, and spend time in the presence of God before my family woke up. I then cooked breakfast for my family and got my children ready and off to school. Once I had my personal time with God and took care of my family's needs, I was able to spend the day studying in depth, memorizing God's Word, and ministering deliverance to women over the phone. I spent hours doing this. I then returned to my household duties: cleaning and preparing meals for my family. I made sure dinner was cooked by the time my husband and children came home.

By this time, testimonies about God restoring my marriage were spreading. Women started calling me asking if they could come to my house on their lunch breaks to get prayer and counsel for their marriage. I would take them downstairs in my basement. I imparted the same deliverance I had received. I commanded and cast out demons. The very same crying and screaming that I had experienced years ago was now coming from my basement. The Holy Spirit was teaching me how to take authority over the demons and command them to get out. The Bible says, "Behold, I give unto you power to tread on serpents and scorpions...and nothing shall by any means hurt you" (Luke 10:19).

I prayed for them and encouraged them to set the atmosphere of their home with love, worship, God's Word, prayer, and holy living. I let them know that these things would help them to maintain their deliverance.

This went on every day for years. I remember a young lady rang my doorbell late one night. She had been abused, like so many of the women that came to my home. She told me what happened and said she had nowhere to go. I prayed for her and then told her about different pastors she could go to for help. When I closed the door with tears in my eyes, the Lord spoke to me and said, "I am sending the women to you. Why are you sending them away?" From then on I opened my house as a healing house of refuge where women could come to receive prayer, deliverance and encouragement. God was showing me His plan, process, and purpose for my life. I see so many people today who are self-appointed. But I didn't go looking for these women——they came looking for me. The Bible says, "A man's gift maketh room for him, and bringeth him before great men" (Prov. 18:16).

Once a month women would gather from far and near for prayer, deliverance, healing, counsel, teaching, and discipleship training. I had developed a lifestyle of prayer, holiness, and deliverance and would always remind the women of that. I let them all know, "If God is sending you here, He is sending you for prayer, holiness, and deliverance." I referred to this combination—prayer, holiness, and deliverance—as my spiritual PhD.

Married Woman

> But she that is married careth for the things of the world, how she may please her husband.
> —1 Corinthians 7:34

So many wives feel like they are not important if they are not standing behind the pulpit with a microphone in their hands. What they may fail to realize is the ministry of a wife comes with a heavy responsibility from God and is just as important as pulpit ministry. Although God can use her in both arenas, she should never feel one role is greater. When we are doing what we were created to do, it pleases the Lord.

In this twenty-first century, not many women embrace the traditional responsibilities of a wife. Many have devalued the ministry of the wife. However, the ministry of a wife is just as important as an apostle, prophet, evangelist, pastor, or teacher. If we look through the spiritual lens, the ministry of a wife functions out of these five-fold ministry gifts. She is a sent one to her family (i.e., an apostle). She prays, preaches, prophesies, and builds up her family, as a prophet does. She witnesses and tells her family, friends, and others about Jesus, functioning as an evangelist. She watches over, tends to, and feeds her family (as a pastor would). She teaches her household the importance of loving God, loving others, serving, and giving. Some women may find it foreign to develop the ministry of a wife: making a happy home for her husband, taking care of his needs, cooking, cleaning, washing, sewing, etc. This may indicate that they are not ready to become wives.

The ministry of a wife is more than being a great wife, a great mother, and one who cooks, cleans, and helps raise the children. The ministry of a wife is a big responsibility. In Genesis 2:18 it says that a wife is to be a helpmate to her husband, one who stands alongside of him. One of the ways you can be helpful to your husband is by praying for him. Pray that he be the man that God has purposed for him to be. Pray for him to be the priest and prophet in his home. Pray that he has favor with God and man. Pray for peace, prosperity, and promotions on his job. Pray for good health and strength. Remember, the ministry of a wife is to pray for her husband and family.

Respect your husband and recognize and acknowledge him as the head of his house. The ministry of a wife is a ministry of submission to God, His Word, and to her husband. As I stated earlier, God will not ask you to submit to something that is not in alignment with His Word, and neither will a godly husband. But unless your husband is asking you to do something that is ungodly, it is wise to support and build your relationship with your husband by showing him respect. The Word says, "Every wise woman buildeth her house: but the foolish plucketh it down with her hands" (Prov. 14:1).

According to 1 Peter 3:1, if your husband is not saved but you are, then he is sanctified through you. Demonstrate God's love to him. It's through love and kindness that God draws us.

Give yourself freely to your husband. (See 1 Corinthians 7:3–5.) Withholding yourself physically or spiritually from him is disobeying the Word of God. It is hard to give yourself to your husband when you are holding unforgiveness in your heart. Make the decision to walk in forgiveness, knowing that God has forgiven you.

Every woman may not be called to stand behind a pulpit in the church, but your house is your pulpit. Your kitchen sink becomes your pulpit. Your dinner table becomes your pulpit. Your living room and bedroom are your pulpit. I know some women may think they are too apostolic and prophetic to fulfill their responsibilities of the ministry of wives, but if you are married you must understand that your first ministry is the ministry of marriage. Build your house with God's presence through prayer, praise, and peace.

The Silent, Secret Sin: Dealing with Spousal Jealousy

> And Deborah, [a governmental woman and] a prophetess, the wife of Lapidoth, she judged Israel at that time. And she dwelt under the palm tree of Deborah between Ramah and Bethel in mount Ephraim: and the children of Israel came up to her for judgment. And she sent and called Barak the son of Abinoam out of Kedeshnaphtali, and said unto him, Hath not the Lord God of Israel commanded, saying, Go and draw toward mount

> Tabor, and take with thee ten thousand men of the children of Naphtali and of the children of Zebulun? And I will draw unto thee to the river Kishon Sisera, the captain of Jabin's army, with his chariots and his multitude; and I will deliver him into thine hand. And Barak said unto her, If thou wilt go with me, then I will go: but if thou wilt not go with me, then I will not go. And she said, I will surely go with thee: notwithstanding the journey that thou takest shall not be for thine honour; for the Lord shall sell Sisera into the hand of a woman. And Deborah arose, and went with Barak to Kedesh.
>
> —JUDGES 4:4–9

Today, we have modern-day women who are prophetesses and judges. Their husbands may be businessmen, lawyers or in different leadership positions. Yet, their wives function in higher leadership roles in the kingdom. This was the case with Deborah and Lapidoth. Deborah was a prophetess and a judge. I believe if Deborah were living in our day and time she may have been the president of her country. She was also the wife of Lapidoth. The scriptures don't indicate that Deborah and her husband served together in a leadership position. I believe that Deborah's husband, Lapidoth, was a leader in some capacity, but they didn't serve together.

When God uses one spouse more than the other, the enemy may cause them to struggle with secret jealousy. This spirit of jealousy has caused separations and divorce. The Bible says, "Jealousy is cruel as the grave" (Song of Sol. 8:6). When you are jealous of someone, you are simply putting them in a grave to bury them while they are still breathing. That is very cruel. When you are feeling jealous of someone, the first step to deliverance is honesty. You must be honest that you are jealous. Confess it, denounce it, repent, and get delivered from it.

To avoid spousal jealousy, it is important not to make your spouse feel less than just because God is using you in a greater way. Although my husband has been very supportive of me in ministry, when God began to open doors for me to go to the nations, it initially bothered me that he did not appear to be excited or happy for me. I would ask him, "What's wrong?" but he would say, "Nothing." I knew he felt left out. I had to learn how important it is to ask your spouse if he would like to assist you in your assignment. Regardless of whom God is using, always remember you are one and are on the same team.

Every spouse may not feel called to the pulpit. They may feel comfortable working behind the scenes or working with children and families.

Some spouses may have fears or feelings of inadequacy. The devil will send silent jealousy to attack their minds when God is using their spouse in a certain way.

Mature men are not intimidated or insecure but can recognize a woman's ability to do something that they may not have the grace to do. Judges 4:8–9 says, "And Barak said to [Deborah]... If thou wilt go with me, then I will go: but if thou wilt not go with me, then I will not go. And she said, I will surely go with thee." Some may think that Barak was a coward because he refused to go without Deborah, but Barak was a general—a military man who understood the importance of having a strategy. He understood rank, position, power, and authority. He understood the favor that Deborah had as a judge.

God is raising men of God like Barak who will recognize the kingdom woman's mandate, mantle, and ministry. They will assist her in her God-given assignment. It does not mean that he is Ahab and she is Jezebel. It simply means whether God gives an assignment to a male or female, He will supply the grace to accomplish His purpose and to advance the kingdom.

UNMARRIED WOMEN

> The unmarried woman careth for the things of the Lord, that she may be holy both in body and in spirit: but she that is married careth for the things of the world, how she may please her husband.
> —1 CORINTHIANS 7:34

The ministry of the unmarried is to care for the things of the Lord, that she may be holy in body and in spirit. Romans 12:1–2 says, "I beseech you therefore, brethren, by the mercies of God, that ye present your bodies a living sacrifice, holy, acceptable unto God, which is your reasonable service. And be not conformed to this world: but be ye transformed by the renewing of your mind, that ye may prove what is that good, and acceptable, and perfect, will of God." In the twenty-first century, it is rare to hear about unmarried women who are holy virgins in body and in spirit. But there are some unmarried women that have taken Romans 12:1–2 to heart. There are six things that constitute the acceptable and perfect will of God demonstrated in the unmarried woman's life:

- She presents her body as a living sacrifice.
- She does not give her body to fornication.

- She makes herself acceptable to God.
- She renders her reasonable service.
- She does not conform to this world.
- She is transformed by the renewing of her mind.

The ministry of the unmarried woman is one of intense sacrifice and focused devotion to God. The supreme call of her life is to develop her relationship with God and bring forth fruit from it for others. Anna the prophetess is a perfect example. In Luke 2:36–37 we read that she was devoted to her relationship to God and her reasonable service of prayer. The unmarried woman spends quality time ministering to the Lord through prayer, fasting, and rendering her service unto the Lord. She may hope to one day embrace the ministry of a wife, however, her primary focus is on pleasing the Lord.

Generational Partnerships

> As iron sharpens iron, so one person sharpens another.
> —Proverbs 27:17, niv

God will send people into your life to sharpen you, no matter how young or how old you are. A midwife is a woman trained to assist women in childbirth: God anoints older and mature kingdom women to function like midwives to train and assist younger kingdom women in fulfilling their call and destiny. I used to think that at sixty years old I was too old to start over again, but the Lord reminded me of the story of Mary and Elizabeth. Mary and Elizabeth were both pregnant, and they were both carrying something great. Mary was carrying Jesus, the Son of God, and Elizabeth was carrying John the Baptist, the forerunner of Jesus. When Elizabeth heard the salutation of Mary, the baby John the Baptist leapt in her womb. (See Luke 1:41.)

Mary thought she was too young to give birth, and Elizabeth thought she was too old to give birth. God sent them to one another to encourage each other. Likewise, God will send people into your life who will see the potential and call on your life. They will cause your baby to leap, your vision to leap, dreams to leap, and they will stay with you until the assignment is done. Get ready, because your baby is about to leap.

Millennials and baby boomers are called to connect and collaborate in the kingdom for just this purpose. Spiritual midwives and spiritual handmaidens from different generations are positioned to help push you into your purpose and destiny. You are not too young or too old to start again. Come on! It's time to push that baby out!

God is sending millennials to baby boomers. The younger will not despise the older. They will not be jealous and envious. Millennials have knowledge of technology that can benefit baby boomers, and the baby boomers have wisdom that can benefit the millennials in their walk with God.

Don't Be a Cover Girl

There are too many issues within the church. Insecurity is one of those issues. Your spiritual DNA is what distinguishes you from women of the world. You don't have to exalt yourself or put other women down to demonstrate your value and worth. A kingdom woman empowers women. Kingdom women embrace and encourage you to soar because kingdom women are in competition with no one. They are ambassadors for God. They are God's gorgeous girls, princesses, daughters of the sovereign King, fearfully and wonderfully made by God. They are kingdom women—the King's daughters.

Kingdom woman, if you are not careful, you will find yourself feeling like you don't measure up to other women. The Bible says those who "compare themselves with one another" (2 Cor. 10:12, ESV) "are not wise" (2 Cor. 10:12, NIV). I'm not opposed to the Cover Girl makeup company, but we do need to steer clear of becoming the cover girl who covers up covetousness, competitions, and hatred in her heart against other women. I'm talking about those who cover up jealousy, envy, strife, bitterness, and unforgiveness. Instead of covering up these negative characteristics, we need to surrender them to the Lord and walk in righteousness. This is what separates kingdom women from ghetto girls. A ghetto girl likes to play games, but a kingdom woman is a game changer. She creates the game. Her sister may have blemishes, but she will cover her sister's scars. She will not uncover her sister's vulnerability. A kingdom woman carries her sister in prayer and intercession. Remember, a kingdom woman is more than a conqueror through Christ. She will not be defeated. A kingdom woman seeks to win in every area of her life, but not at the expense of others.

Kingdom women value their virtue. The kingdom woman is a woman of wisdom, power, and influence. She is not intimidated by ghetto girls who are territorial and say, "This is my turf. This is my square. And I'm not going to allow any new kids on the block to have my stuff because I was here first." That's a worldly mentality. At the same time, a kingdom woman does not ask permission when God is leading her to possess new land. She understands "the kingdom of heaven suffereth violence, and the violent take it by force" (Matt. 11:12). She uses her weapons of prayer, praise and worship, and submission to God's Word. She is a warrior.

The enemy likes to point out the mistakes you've made in the past. Don't cover your pain with Cover Girl makeup. God can turn your pain to power.

Likewise, there is no amount of makeup that can cover up your bad attitude. Your attitude will determine your altitude. It doesn't matter how anointed or how gifted and talented you are; if you do not walk in godly character, integrity, and the fruit of the Spirit, the works you do will all be in vain.

God is asking us to be a new type of cover girl—a cover girl who will cover her sister in prayer. We must be willing to look past what she may be wearing. We must look past how well her makeup is done. We must look past how beautiful she looks on the outside and pray for her inward struggles. She has a covenant with the Lord, and she has a covenant with her sisters. So cover girl, cover your sister in sisterhood and "pray one for another, that ye may be healed" (James 5:16).

Chapter 10

THE KINGDOM WOMAN PREPARING FOR FIVEFOLD MINISTRY

*Therefore seeing we have this ministry, as we
have received mercy, we faint not.*
—2 Corinthians 4:1

Your ministry will come out of your relationship with God. God must always be first in your ministry. Character and integrity are very important in ministry, along with practicing a godly lifestyle. Your ministry needs to be submitted to your leadership. God will use natural gifts, but you must always surrender your gift to God.

People often struggle with their identity, especially women. Some are not happy about the way they look or their personality. As a result, they try to alter who God has made them to be. They begin to compare themselves with other women. The Bible says, "For we dare not make ourselves of the number, or compare ourselves with some that commend themselves: but they measuring themselves by themselves, and comparing themselves among themselves, are not wise" (2 Cor. 10:12).

When God began to use me in ministry, I noticed there was a strong force I felt on the inside. It was indescribable. This reminded me of a dream I had in which the Spirit of the Lord came upon me, and my voice sounded like a trumpet. The words would come forth strong, with great power. Once I began to minister, my voice would become strong and authoritative as the anointing was upon me. God has given me a very unique and distinctive voice. But I would often hold back that anointing I was feeling on the inside so that I would not appear different. I didn't realize I was neglecting the gift God had given me by holding back. Similarly, God would often give me prophetic illustrations to use while I preached, yet because I didn't see many others being used that way, I was reluctant to use the different illustrations. This was another way I was neglecting the gift that was given to me. I would go to God and pray, "Lord, change the way I minister. Don't let my voice come across so strong and loud." It wasn't that the people were not receptive; it was me comparing my God-given gift to those He had given to others.

Psalm 29:4 says, "The voice of the LORD is powerful; the voice of the LORD is full of majesty." When God uses you, it's not you but God's power flowing through you. It's OK to be different as long as you are not walking around looking spooky and acting goofy.

I am an introvert. I'm quiet, and I don't talk much, but I have learned to embrace the fact that when the anointing comes, it changes me into a different person, like it says in 1 Samuel 10:6: "The Spirit of the LORD will come powerfully upon you, and you will prophesy with them. You will be changed into a different person" (NLT).

People often relate to me as the lion and the lamb. At times I roar like a lion, but other times I'm meek like a lamb. That's all part of God's design for me.

What am I saying? Your destiny is too important for you to deny the person God has created you to be. Remember, you were made in the likeness and the image of God, not in the likeness and the image of someone else. Stop comparing yourself with others! Be a confident woman! Be yourself! Be comfortable in who God has made you to be! He has made you an original, so stop trying to be a carbon copy of someone else. Love the woman that God has created you to be. Partner with the Holy Spirit, and He will help you flow in the gifts of the Spirit. The Holy Spirit will lead you and guide you into all truth. The Holy Spirit will teach and train you. So don't neglect the gift!

Your Gift Will Make Room for You

So many people try to push their way into the pulpit, but you don't have to push your way in. Remember, the Bible says your gift will make room for you and bring you "before great men" (Prov. 18:16). There are some churches that already have people in key positions, and you may feel there is no room for your gift. Kingdom woman, don't give up or give in to the temptation to try to get ahead by putting yourself before others. Apostolic, kingdom women do not suffer from crabs-in-a-barrel syndrome, pulling other women down to pull herself up. A kingdom woman does not try to make room for herself, because her gift, which has been given by God, will make room for her.

In my earlier walk with the Lord I was at a church service, and the pastor called me out and began to prophesy over me. The pastor said, "The anointing is upon your life, and I see the fire of God all around you." The pastor went on to say, "The Lord said, 'When you open your mouth I will fill it. You shall preach the gospel, and you shall prophesy.' God said, 'I call you a prophet to the nations.'" I didn't understand what all of that meant at the time, but the Lord reminded me of a word He had spoken many years ago, which said that He was going to use me to preach the gospel.

I was in shock that words like that were spoken with power and authority over me. I begged the person who rode with me to church that night not to tell anyone about what happened in the service, not even my family. To be honest, I had a hard time believing that God had a calling on my life. If I didn't even believe it fully, I definitely wasn't sure if my family would believe that God was calling me into ministry. No one that I knew in my family was in ministry at the time. Nonetheless, each time I would go to church it seemed like God was illuminating prophetic words for me. These words were constantly being released over me. However, this took place in the eighties, and needless to say those prophetic words have come to pass. His words "shall not return unto…[Him] void" (Isa. 55:11).

> God is not a man, that He should lie; neither the son of man, that he should repent.
> —Numbers 23:19

> The Lord said…"I am watching over my word to perform it."
> —Jeremiah 1:12, esv

In my early years in church, I was often called on to pray or bring forth a ten- or fifteen-minute message. I was about thirty years old the first time I was invited to be a guest speaker. I had received a ministry certificate, but I was not ordained. A neighborhood pastor was running a revival, and one of the ladies of his church requested that I be the Sunday morning speaker. The pastor didn't know me, but he had heard the call of God was on my life. This was amazing, because some pastors will only invite well-known ministers to speak at their church.

The service was in a small storefront Pentecostal church. I was excited but very nervous. It was my first time being a guest speaker, and I was just a babe in Christ. I didn't know what I should preach about, so I prayed and asked the Lord, but He didn't answer. Then, I had a dream that I had a fruit basket, and I was giving people different kinds of fruit. When I woke up I felt that the fruit of the spirit was what the Lord wanted me to preach about, so I went to the store and bought the biggest fruit basket I could afford. That service I preached from the fifth chapter of Galatians. The message was fiery. After I was finished preaching I made an altar call, and as I began to pray for the people I would give them some fruit, as the Lord led. (I now know that it was the spirit of prophecy operating through prophetic illustrations.) As I continued to minister to people at the altar, many people were falling out before I could give them the fruit. I was amazed by the power of God.

The pastor told me how blessed he was and asked me to come back. He handed me a large yellow envelope and said, "We want to give you an honorarium." I immediately handed it back to him and said, "No, I don't preach for money." In fact, I didn't know people received money for preaching. He said, "I know, daughter. We want to be a blessing to you." I told him, "That's OK; just sow it into your ministry."

When I got into the car my husband was so proud of me. He said, "God really blessed you. You were a blessing to the people." Then he asked, "Did the pastor give you an honorarium?" Pentecostal services back then were usually very long services, and he and the kids were hungry and hoping we could go out to dinner. I said, "Yes, but I gave it back." He replied, "You did what?" I repeated, "I said I gave it back for him to put into the ministry." Several minutes of silence followed. I started to think that I should have kept it. My husband finally said, "God will bless you for that."

Later on I was still questioning my decision. I wondered if it was an unwise decision, considering that we lived off one income. I soon heard the Lord say, "I can trust you." In ministry, the devil will tempt you, but God will test you. Put your trust in the Lord. Jehovah Jireh is your provider. You must know that when you "give...it will be given [back] to you. Good measure, pressed down, shaken together, running over, will be put into your lap" (Luke 6:38, ESV).

I remember the second time I was invited to speak at the same church. I was seeking the Lord on what He wanted me to share. I had another dream, and in the dream, I was in the water with all these beautiful fish of different colors. There were all different kinds of fish. The dream led me to preach a message from the passage of scripture when Jesus said, "I will make you fishers of men." (See Matthew 4:19.) The Holy Spirit instructed me to get a fishing pole, a tackle box, and bait to use as illustrations. After I was finished preaching I had an altar call. Several young people and adults came up and gave their lives to the Lord. Hallelujah!

Although God may give you a gift to minister, God will make you in the process. You must be willing to allow God to make you according to His image and likeness.

> Those that be planted in the house of the LORD shall flourish in the courts of our God.
> —PSALM 92:13

I ORDAINED YOU

> Then the word of the LORD came unto me, saying, Before I formed thee in the belly I knew thee; and before thou camest forth out of the womb I sanctified thee, and I ordained thee a prophet unto the nations. Then said I, Ah, LORD God! behold, I cannot speak: for I am a child. But the LORD said unto me, Say not, I am a child: for thou shalt go to all that I shall send thee, and whatsoever I command thee thou shalt speak. Be not afraid of their faces: for I am with thee to deliver thee, saith the LORD. Then the LORD put forth his hand, and touched my mouth. And the LORD said unto me, Behold, I have put my words in thy mouth. See, I have this day set thee over the nations and over the kingdoms, to root out, and to pull down, and to destroy, and to throw down, to build, and to plant.
> —JEREMIAH 1:4–10

I believe before you are ordained in the natural, God has already ordained you in the Spirit. Kingdom woman, when you feel nervous about stepping out into the ministry to which God has called you, remember to be bold and courageous, because your God will always be faithful to "carry out all... [His] plans" for you (Jer. 1:12, NLT). The Bible says that "God's gifts and his call are irrevocable" (Rom. 11:29, NIV). When God calls you and ordains you, He will not fail to equip you. He will open doors that no man can shut, and He will speak, leading and guiding you to keep you on the path He has laid out for you. (See Isaiah 30:21.)

I received a prophetic word in the year 2000 that I was going to receive ordination papers and that the nations were calling me. This seemed impossible in the natural, but I trusted God and was faithful to continue to walk in obedience and get myself ready. In 2001, I was ordained as a prophet, and God began to open doors to the nations.

The nation of China (2001)

I had a dream while I was in Georgia preaching at a conference. In the dream, the streets were filled with people dancing at what looked like some kind of festival, and I saw Asian people under a dragon-type image. I didn't understand why I would have a dream like that.

When I got back to church in Chicago on Sunday one of the prophets asked me if I was going on the church's mission trip to China. I said I didn't currently have plans to go, but I believed I was supposed to. I told her that I had just had a dream that I was in China. I described the dream to her. I told her about the Asian people under a dragon dancing. She said in China every year during their holiday season they have a festival in the streets. She then told me that she believed that I was supposed to go too. She told me that the deadline to sign up had passed, but she would check to see if anyone had backed out.

That's exactly what happened! Someone backed out. Not only did God give me grace to go, but I later found out my trip was paid for in full. I was so excited, because no one in my family had ever gone to the nations. I was chosen by the Lord to be the first in my family to go to the nations.

Sometime before our trip I received a call from the team leader for the trip to China. She said, "I'm glad you are going. I know you are strong in deliverance, and I would like you to be the captain of the deliverance team." Although the Lord had been training me for years in deliverance, I was nervous. I had just recently joined the church and didn't think I was qualified for such a position. On top of it, not everyone on the team was happy about the leadership decision. However, the Bible reminds us that God will equip us for the call, and we must be mindful that promotion does not come from man but from God.

When we got to China I could hardly believe it, but I was seeing the very thing I dreamed about before my eyes. It was China's holiday season. The streets were filled with people dancing, and I saw that dragon. It was almost everywhere I looked. It was on walls, billboards, pictures, and other places. It was a prominent part of their celebration. That dragon costume was part of the Chinese festival. I decided to take God giving me that dream—which included something I was not aware of— as a confirmation that it was one of my assignments to go to China. This was especially significant to me when I began to experience spiritual warfare while I was there. It taught me a crucial lesson: Don't allow challenges to cause you to change your mind concerning God's assignment for your life. Be assured, whom the Lord calls He also qualifies for the work.

Our deliverance ministry there was crazy, but exciting

to me. Witchcraft was really strong where we were. We prayed for people and cast demons out of people from ten o'clock in the morning to four or five o'clock in the evening. I remember two deliverance ministers working with a very tiny woman. The demons in her were giving the workers a rough time. They were struggling with that woman a long time. As I watched and prayed in tongues the Lord gave me a word of knowledge. I went over to that tiny women and very quietly whispered in her ear, "Spirits of rape and molestation come out of her in the name of Jesus." The woman's body rose up from the floor (levitated), and she pointed to me and said with a loud voice, "She said it. She said it." We later found out that her pastor, several men in the church, and others had raped and molested her. Being led by God brought great deliverance in that woman's life and the lives of many others.

China will never be the same because Jesus came and set the captives free. Glory to God!

The nation of South Africa (2003)

I am still amazed to see dreams and destiny being fulfilled in my life. God asked me the question, "Whom shall I send?" Like the prophet Isaiah, I responded to the call by saying, "Send me, I will go." (See Isaiah 6:8.)

One day I was at home just finishing my time of prayer and studying the Word of God when I received a phone call. The person was calling to invite me to go to South Africa. This trip also was completely paid for. I was both excited and nervous.

When I got to Africa, I fell in love with the continent and the people. We went to church that first night, and after the service the host pastor asked me to close out in prayer. The next morning the pastor took us to the top of the mountains to pray. This was so exciting. While standing on top of a rock when I was in South Africa I remembered a dream I had years before about Luke 4:18 coming to pass in my life, and I was deeply moved.

After prayer, the pastor took us around to introduce us. I will never forget one of the older mothers from the church. I could tell she was a praying woman. She pulled me aside and said to me, "You are one of the speakers?" I replied, "No, ma'am, I came to assist the speaker." This little old lady was so sure of herself. She said, "You are the speaker. I saw your face on posters." I just smiled, but the next day the pastor said to me, "I sense you are carrying something great. I would like you to speak in the conference." I was really nervous, but I knew this was God's divine plan for my life.

I went to my room that night praying and seeking God about what He wanted me to share. I saw a vision of gift boxes wrapped with beautiful bows. The next day I asked one of the women if they would go to the store to get me some gift boxes. Each box represented the fivefold gifts in Ephesians 4:11–12: "And He gave some, apostles; and some, prophets; and some, evangelists; and some, pastors and teachers; For the perfecting of the saints, for the work of the ministry, for the edifying of the body of Christ." When I preached that message, the power of God was phenomenal. I had never prophesied to that many people in all my life.

God blessed me to go back to South Africa again, and the power of God was even stronger. That time I preached a message titled "Keys to the Kingdom." God gave me a prophetic song, "Let the Lion Roar; Let the Eagle Soar." That was the first time I had ever experienced that kind of anointing on my life. I gave each of the pastors and leaders kingdom keys as a prophetic demonstration, and as they took them they begin to fall under the power of God. It was still a surprise to experience the power of God coming out of my mouth when there was a time I was too afraid to stand before people. Even today, after all He has done through my life and ministry, I remain in awe of His power and decision to choose me as His mouthpiece.

I have been to South Africa several times, and each time God has used me in a powerful way. I love Africa. It will always be like a second home for me.

The nation of Germany (2007)

In 2007, I went with a team to Germany to attend a pastor's conference. We had a great time, and after the conference ended some of the German pastors asked a few of the guest speakers to come to their churches and speak on Sunday morning. The guest speakers were catching a plane that night after the conference but gave instructions to invite two of the ordained leaders from our team to go in their stead. Surprisingly, another ordained prophet from our church and I were chosen to go preach! I had never met the pastors who invited me to come, and they had never heard me preach before. But there I was, preparing to speak to their congregation. This was truly a divine door opened. It just demonstrates that you don't have to push your way to achieve the destiny God has for you. The Bible says your gift will make room for you (Prov. 18:16).

When I arrived at the church on Sunday morning to preach, I was introduced to the pastor of the church, who was a woman. Personally, I was so excited to know another woman pastor. Her church was a castle.

I preached a message on the fire of God. I'm always amazed at the power of God and how He shows up. When I got back home the pastor called to ask if I would come back. I was excited to be invited back again.

The second time I was in Germany, while I was preaching, uniformed military persons came in and stood at the back door with machine guns (they were probably the equivalent to our National Guard). I was so radical, I kept preaching. When the anointing of God is on you, there is no fear. After the service, the pastor told me there was a high alert due to terrorism and there had been a bomb threat. Somehow they knew I was not from Germany, and I had to show them my identification. They checked everything, including my driver's car, and everything was put on lockdown. I was not allowed to leave my hotel room. I began to pray asking God to send angels to protect me. I am thankful to God I didn't get gunned down while I was preaching. Sometimes your life can be put at risk preaching the gospel, so it's important to put your trust in God and to make sure it's God ordering your steps. A good man's footsteps are ordered by the Lord.

The nation of India (2005)

After my trip to South Africa I was invited to go with a team from my church to India. When we got to the airport in India I was getting a cart to put my luggage on. I didn't see a piece of rusted steel and cut my finger so deeply that it bled on and off the entire time I was in India. I felt like it was an attack from the enemy to hinder my assignment. We had a nurse on our team who treated my wound every day. Still, there were so many attacks on this trip that I began to question if I was in the will of God. It is in these instances that you must stay focused and walk in faith.

When we went to the crusade there were so many people at the crusade who were sick and believing God for miracles. I too was in need of a healing. Nevertheless, after I finished preaching, a woman brought her son to me to pray for him. She said he was born deaf. Fear gripped my heart. I was thinking, "What if I pray for him, and he doesn't get healed?" I closed my eyes and put my finger inside the boy's ears and prayed the prayer of faith.

Even as I prayed for this boy, another man came up to me and took my hand and laid it on his stomach. He had stomach cancer. As we prayed, miracles started happening. People were coming up to share their testimonies. We actually saw a man who was lame from birth walk.

After the meeting was over, I heard the mother of the deaf boy screaming and saying, "My son can hear! My son can hear!" All I could think and pray was, "Glory to God! He is the God who heals!"

That night I preached again. There was so many demonic manifestations—witchcraft and people with deformities (no legs, no feet, large tumors sticking out of their bodies), people screaming, and doing all kinds of weird things that actually scared me too, though I knew that I couldn't show any sign of fear. The manifestations increased, so I stopped preaching and called the prayer team together to start praying for the sick.

The minute I laid my hands on one lady, she fell to the ground and her eyes rolled completely in the back of her head. All that was visible were the white parts of her eyes. People were screaming, "You killed her! You killed her!" There are no words to describe how scared I was. All I could think of was, "What if this woman is really dead?" God gave me a word of knowledge that there was a spirit of witchcraft and I also began to bind the spirit of death (Matt. 18:18). Soon, her eyes came back to normal, and she got up clapping her hands, shouting, and dancing. I had never experienced anything like that before, but it most definitely left an impact in my life. To God be the glory.

As a kingdom woman, you develop an extreme faith that comes from being faithful to the Father in whatever time and place He calls you to bring the power of the kingdom to the people who need it most.

The nation of Zimbabwe (2013)

One morning after prayer, I turned my cell on and saw I had received a message in my inbox on social media. The message was from a pastor in Zimbabwe. I didn't know then that he was the same pastor God had used me to prophesy to when I was in South Africa. He asked if I would come to Zimbabwe, as he was hosting their first women's conference and wanted me to be one of the speakers. He explained that all expenses would be paid. I was so excited. This was the first time God Himself opened a major door for me supernaturally. Up until that point, I had been asked to be a part of teams, but now I would be taking a team to the nations. People were coming from Kenya, Tanzania, Zambia, Uganda, and South Africa. I was excited about the assignment from God, but I was also afraid of the unknown.

I began fasting and praying for this assignment weeks in advance. I sought God for a message for Zimbabwe. I heard the Lord say, "Jezebel." I did not give it any thought, but it stayed in my spirit. When I would prepare to study, the Lord would impress upon my heart to study the spirit of Jezebel. I believe that was the message God wanted me to give in Zimbabwe, but I wrestled with God, thinking, "Here it is that You have opened a major door for the first time, and You want me to speak about Jezebel?" He reminded me about the dream I had many years ago in which I saw the word *Ashtaroth*. She was an ancient goddess who many believed to be the queen of heaven. Even with the reminder about that dream, I still didn't want to preach about Jezebel. I wanted to preach about someone like Esther or Deborah, apostolic women.

I thought, "What if they don't ask me to come back?" If we are not careful we, as preachers, will preach smooth messages, preaching what the people want to hear. The Bible says God's sheep "know his voice. And a stranger will they not follow" (John 10:4–5). You may not be popular when you preach penetrating messages from God, but remember, "obedience is better than sacrifice" or the approval of man (1 Sam. 15:22, NLT).

The moral of the story is that in spite of the fact that I came under several witchcraft attacks, uncontrollable nose bleeding, demonic dreams of dying, and other things, I obeyed God. I obeyed God in spite of the looks on some of their faces. The Bible says to "set...[your] face like a flint" (Isa. 50:7). I faced the fear and walked by faith. Sometimes you've got to do it afraid.

The pastor came to me after service and said, "This is it. This is what we have been dealing with, the spirit of Jezebel." Other pastors came forward telling me the same thing. The apostle Paul said, "Am I to obey God or man?" (Acts 5:29, author's paraphrase), and that attitude was my guide. In the end, the pastor invited me to come back to Zimbabwe. I did, and this time the assignment was even greater.

Overcoming fear can be challenging, but like David, you must have confidence to kill the lion and the bear and the Goliaths to have victory. There may be a time in your life that you may face life-threatening situations, but a kingdom woman learns how to become strong in the Lord and decree and declare, "I shall not die, but live, and declare the works of the Lord" (Ps. 118:17).

Covered by God

> And I will give you shepherds after my own heart, who will feed you with knowledge and understanding.
> —Jeremiah 3:15, esv

There are some women who believe they can't be in a place of authority because the husband is the head, but I would have you know that "the head of every man is Christ; and the head of the woman is the man; and the head of Christ is God" (1 Cor. 11:3). And if some women do minister, they believe they should not minister without wearing a head covering. However, the Bible tells us that Christ is our covering. While a literal head covering may not be necessary, it is wise to minister under the spiritual covering of a pastor, mentor, or other leader.

Not having a pastor or covering has become an issue in the kingdom. You should have someone to whom you can be accountable, someone who can feed you knowledge and understanding and even correct you when you are wrong. Jeremiah 3:15 promises, "And I will give you pastors according to mine heart, which shall feed you with knowledge and understanding." Hebrews 13:17 says, "Obey them that have the rule over you, and submit yourselves: for they watch for your souls, as they that must give account, that they may do it with joy, and not with grief: for that is unprofitable for you."

There are some people who have a struggle with submitting to and obeying those who have rule over them. They may lack revelation concerning submission to God's Word. I'm not talking about pastors who are controlling. There is a difference between a person who has concerns for your best interests and those who want to control you. But many leaders do not want to submit to a pastor because of past experiences with controlling pastors. If you believe God has called you to be in a place of authority, it's important to get healed from any past hurts, including wounds related to church leadership. The Bible says, "Be ye clean, that bear the vessels of the Lord" (Isa. 52:11).

There are still some people who do not believe in women pastors or leaders. They may or may not recognize the call of God on your life. They may not release you to flow in your gifts. They may never ordain you into your office. My pastor has shared his testimony how he came from a traditional background and had struggles in ordaining women in a fivefold office. God has given him revelation of His Word, and he has since ordained and released countless women to flow in their gifts and callings.

It is important to find a pastor or spiritual mentor who has discernment and can see when the character of Christ has not been fully developed in a person. That person should be able to tell you to wait until they see your gift has been tried and proven by God and men, or to release you into your ministry when it is time.

Chapter 11

THE KINGDOM WOMAN SERVING IN FIVEFOLD MINISTRY

Neglect not the gift that is in thee, which was given thee by prophecy, with the laying on of the hands of the presbytery.
—1 Timothy 4:14

In a previous chapter we talked about a couple of scriptures that cause some to question whether or not women should be in ministry. Now that we have established that God does desire for women to lead in ministry, it's time to focus on biblical examples of women active in the fivefold ministry gifts:

> And he gave some, apostles; and some, prophets; and some, evangelists; and some, pastors and teachers; For the perfecting of the saints, for the work of the ministry, for the edifying of the body of Christ.
> —Ephesians 4:11–12

THE KINGDOM WOMAN AS APOSTLE

> And God hath set some in the church, first apostles, secondarily prophets, thirdly teachers, after that miracles, then gifts of healings, helps, governments, diversities of tongues. Are all apostles? are all prophets? are all teachers? are all workers of miracles? Have all the gifts of healing? do all speak with tongues? do all interpret?
> —1 CORINTHIANS 12:28–30

Romans 16:7 lists a woman, Junia, as an apostle: "Salute Andronicus and Junia, my kinsmen, and my fellow-prisoners, who are of note among the apostles, who also were in Christ before me." Author Hakeem Collins writes, "The Greek word *apostolos*, from which we derive the word *apostle*, literally means 'one who is sent forth.'"[1] An apostle is someone on mission who represents the one he or she serves.

Were there women disciples?

If Jesus wanted women to minister, how come all His disciples were men? This question is actually raised from a misunderstanding of the word "disciple." Jesus had many women disciples. These include, Mary and Martha (John 11:1–4, and many other references as well. Mary and Martha, along with their brother Lazarus were among Jesus's closest friends). In addition, Jesus had many other women followers as well.

And it came to pass afterward, that he went throughout every city and village, preaching and shewing the glad tidings of the kingdom of God: and the twelve were with him, And certain women, which had been healed of evil spirits and infirmities, Mary called Magdalene, out of whom went seven devils, And Joanna the wife of Chuza Herod's steward, and Susanna, and many others, which ministered unto him of their substance.

—LUKE 8:1–3

For the sake of brevity, I will not include other lists of names of women who followed Him. However the Scriptures make it clear there were many of them.

In another incident, Jesus motions to the crowds that followed him and said, "Behold my mother and my brethren! For whosoever shall do the will of my Father which is in heaven, the same is my brother, and sister, and mother" (Matthew 12:49–50).

In John 4:1–42, we see that it is a Samaritan woman who leads a large population of her community to Jesus.

Why didn't Jesus choose any women to be among His twelve original apostles? Jesus could not choose women to be among the twelve because it would not be wisdom for men and women to be travelling about together when many of them were single. Also, the twelve apostles fulfilled the "type and shadow" of the twelve patriarchs, so they had to be equal to men (Rev. 21:12, 14). However, this doesn't mean that he does not anoint women to fill an apostolic role today, as we already established in the case of Junia.

Jesus showed a great deal of respect for women– and children as well. In the culture of Jesus's day, these were often deemed "lower class" so to speak, and not worth paying serious attention to. However, Jesus repeatedly broke this unspoken rule. Because His actions were so unusual, those closest to Him were often surprised and annoyed.[2]

Apostolic team

No matter how anointed you are, when you have been called into ministry you need an apostolic team to help you carry out the assignment. No one can do ministry alone. We see here that Jesus chose a team to assist Him in His assignment. You too must choose an apostolic team. Again, you cannot do ministry by yourself. The days of a one-man show are over. You must develop a team.

Yes, assembling a team may mean you may encounter a Judas, who may betray you, and a Peter, who may deny you, as they did Jesus. I have been betrayed and denied more than once. It left me feeling devastated and almost caused me to leave my God-given assignment. When that happens, you may share the thoughts of Jesus when He said, "Remove this cup from me: but nevertheless not my will, but thine, be done" (Luke 22:42). When you have been betrayed and denied you must receive healing, deliverance, and forgiveness. Don't allow disappointments in ministry to cause you not to trust anyone. God will put the right people in place to help you minister to the multitudes.

Let's look at Jesus'ss apostolic team of twelve disciples:

> And when he had called unto him his twelve disciples, he gave them power against unclean spirits, to cast them out, and to heal all manner of sickness and all manner of disease. Now the names of the twelve apostles are these; The first, Simon, who is called Peter, and Andrew his brother; James the son of Zebedee, and John his brother; Philip, and

Bartholomew; Thomas, and Matthew the publican; James the son of Alphaeus, and Lebbaeus, whose surname was Thaddaeus; Simon the Canaanite, and Judas Iscariot, who also betrayed him.
—MATTHEW 10:1–4

Here we are told who the disciples were. Each person on the team had a certain role, though they were all His disciples and Christ-ordained to be His apostles or ambassadors.

Apostolic teamwork makes the gospel dream work

Teamwork makes the dream work. Whether you are considering pastoring a church, leading a women's ministry, or opening a business, make sure you understand the requirements. Do not assume that all you need to start a successful ministry is a preaching anointing. In the same way, don't assume that all you need to establish a successful business is a college degree. It is imperative to develop a team. Ministry and business leaders alike can end up burnt out, unsuccessful, and with no growth because they did not build a strong team.

You need economic support, social support, spiritual support, and more. Each person on your team should know how to handle authority and have talents to help build the work. There are some people in leadership who abuse their authority, so don't give novices authority because they may abuse it.

> To give men authority to teach others, that have not ability, is but a mockery to God and the church. It is like, "sending a message by the hand of a fool" (Prov. 26:6). Christ taught his disciples before he sent them forth (Matt. 5:2), and afterwards when

he enlarged their commission he gave them more ample instructions" (Acts 1:3)....

(1) By taking them to be with him. Note, The best preparative for the work of the ministry, is an acquaintance and communion with Jesus Christ. They that would serve Christ must first be with him (John 12:26). Paul had Christ revealed, not only to him but in him, before he went to preach him among the Gentiles, Gal. 1:16. By the lively acts of faith, and the frequent exercise of prayer and meditation, that fellowship with Christ must be maintained and kept up, which is a requisite qualification for the work of the ministry.

(2) By teaching them; they were with him as scholars or pupils and he taught them privately besides the benefit they derived from his public preaching; he opened the scriptures to them and opened their understandings to understand the scriptures: to them it was given to know the mysteries of the kingdom of heaven, and to them they were made plain. Note: They that design to be teachers must first be learners; they must receive that they may give; they must be able to teach others, 2 Tim. 2:2. Gospel truths must be first committed to them before they be commissioned to be gospel ministers.[3]

THE KINGDOM WOMAN AS PROPHET

Along with the ministry of the apostle, the ministry of the prophet is one that is much misunderstood.

> And it shall come to pass afterward, that I will pour out my spirit upon all flesh; and your sons and your daughters shall prophesy, your old men shall dream dreams, your young men shall see

visions: And also upon the servants and upon the handmaids in those days will I pour out my spirit.
—Joel 2:28–29

And he gave some, apostles; and some, prophets.
—Ephesians 4:11

And God hath set some in the church, first apostles, secondarily prophets.
—1 Corinthians 12:28

Author Hakeem Collins writes:

> The New Testament Greek word for prophecy is *propheteuo* and means "to foretell events, divine, speak under inspiration, exercise the prophetic office; to proclaim a divine revelation, prophecy, to foretell the future; to speak forth by divine inspiration; to break forth under sudden impulse or in praise of the divine counsel of God."[4]

Another commentator explains it this way:

> The most basic definition of the Greek word we translate "prophet" is "one who speaks for a god and interprets the god's will." Prophets speak the word of God or announce a word from God.
>
> Prophets apply the apostolic understanding to the situation in which we find ourselves here and now. They speak a word from God that honors what God has done to bring us to where we are and calls forth new possibilities to move us to a new place. When we have become frozen in patterns and habits that are merely repeats of the past, the prophetic word unfreezes us so that we

might move again. We all become stuck. The prophetic word set us free.[5]

It's stated that God spoke to His people by the ministry of the prophets, but all whom God pours His Spirit upon (men and women) will have the ability to prophesy. We may all prophesy, but not all are prophets. A prophet is a person who has been chosen to speak for God, a person who is given a distinctive ministry of representing God before man. He or she is God's mouthpiece or spokesman through which the word of God flows, whether forth-telling or foretelling. A prophet is one who is a seer, one who forth-tells the future. The spirit of prophecy is edification, exhortation, and comfort.

Anna the prophetess is a woman mentioned in the Gospel of Luke. She was an elderly Jewish woman who prophesied about Jesus at the temple of Jerusalem. Anna was eighty-four years old and still praying and prophesying in the temple. (See Luke 2:37.) You may be up in age and feel like you are too old to accomplish your goals, but don't let age come between you and your destiny. Let the aged women arise, pray, teach, preach, prophesy, and impart to the next generation.

A prophetic woman of God has no desire to flow out of her flesh. Her desire is to flow in the Spirit. The word *spirit* represents the breath of God, or *pneuma*—the wind that gives you the ability to flow in the gifts of the Spirit.

A prophetic woman does more than waiting on a microphone and a platform. Much of what she does is done in the secret place. She prays, intercedes, worships, studies, casts out devils, lays hands on the sick, preaches, gives prophecy, and helps others discover their mandate, mantle, ministry, purpose, and destiny. A prophetic woman walks in power, glory, authority, wisdom, knowledge, understanding, revelation, love, and compassion. A prophetic woman carries the mandate of a kingdom woman. In fact, prophets are a reflection of a kingdom woman. They both demonstrate the kingdom.

God's Spirit is not limited to gender but to everyone who will yield to His Spirit. What was God's purpose in pouring out His spirit on *all* flesh? His purpose was for sons and daughters to prophesy and preach the gospel. It was for men and women to flow in the supernatural gifts and impart into the lives of others. God did not leave anyone out when He made the promise through the prophet Joel that He would pour out His "Spirit upon all flesh" (Joel 2:28).

There are women all around the world who may sense the call of God on their lives to speak the word of the Lord to their generation. They are like hidden treasures in the earth. These women have been secretly crying out for ministry. They are saying, "Come over into Macedonia, and help us" (Acts 16:9).

A prophetic woman will challenge women and men to come out of their traditional ways of thinking and fully embrace the Word of God. When God says He will pour out His spirit upon all flesh, that means everyone who yields to the Holy Spirit will be given the ability to pray, preach, prophesy, heal the sick, to raise the dead, and to cast out devils. Freely you have received, so freely give. Take the limits off of God and take the limits off of yourself. Receive a new outpouring of the Holy Spirit and become the kingdom woman that God has ordained you to be.

The Kingdom Woman as Evangelist

> And he gave some, apostles; and some, prophets; and some, evangelists.
> —Ephesians 4:11

The Greek word *euaggelistés* means "preacher or messenger of the Good News." An evangelist is a person with a distinctive ministry who is a bearer of the message of the good news of the saving gospel of Christ. The evangelist is the messenger who preaches, publishes, brings, bears, and carries good tidings. Evangelists also rebuke to bring people to repentance to receive revival and restoration.

Even in the period of the early church, women, as well as men, were considered credible witnesses to the gospel and were commissioned to preach. Mary Magdalene was one who proclaimed the good news of the gospel. Jesus commissioned Mary Magdalene to proclaim His resurrection: "Go to my brothers and say to them, 'I am ascending to my Father and your Father, to my God and your God" (John 20:17, ESV). Mary returned to Jerusalem to proclaim that she had seen the Lord, and she told them that he had said these things to her. Mary Magdalene was the first preacher of the good news of the Resurrection. She preached to the same men who had just been at the tomb.

The Kingdom Woman as Pastor

> And he gave some, apostles; and some, prophets; and some, evangelists; and some, pastors.
> —Ephesians 4:11

> There is neither Jew nor Greek, there is neither slave nor free, there is no male and female, for you are all one in Christ Jesus.
> —Galatians 3:28 ESV

The Greek word for "pastor" is *poimen*, which is translated as "shepherd."[6] It should not be surprising that a pastor is one who tends to flocks, feeding and guiding them. A pastor can also be identified as a servant in the church.

A pastor exercises oversight of the flock of God, the believers. However, all pastors are not apostles, prophets, evangelists, or teachers. There are certain people who have a distinct pastoral call. In contrast to the ministries of the apostle and prophet, the pastoral ministry has been accepted over the centuries.

Phoebe was a pastor of the early church:

> I commend unto you Phebe our sister, which is a servant of the church which is at Cenchrea: That ye receive her in the Lord, as becometh saints, and that ye assist her in whatsoever business she hath need of you: for she hath been a succourer of many, and of myself also.
> —Romans 16:1–2

THE KINGDOM WOMAN AS TEACHER

> And he gave some, apostles; and some, prophets; and some, evangelists; and some, pastors and teachers.
> —Ephesians 4:11

> God hath set some in the church… thirdly teachers.
> —1 Corinthians 12:28–29

> There is neither Jew nor Greek, there is neither bond nor free, there is neither male nor female: for ye are all one in Christ Jesus.
> —GALATIANS 3:28

The Greek word *didasko* is translated "to teach, to learn."[7] The word *teach* means "to impart knowledge and to give instruction."[8] A teacher "is one who points out by the finger, directs, informs, instructs, shoots as an archer, and shows, by teaching the ways of the Lord. His teaching is to flow like water, and comes down like rain."[9]

A teacher is one who is skillful in instruction and causes others to learn. The Bible says this is one of the important functions of older women in the church. Their teaching is like a rod that causes women of God to be "chaste, keepers at home, good, obedient to their own husbands, that the word of God be not blasphemed" (Titus 2:5).

Chapter 12

THE KINGDOM WOMAN: A LEGACY OF INFLUENCE

The involvement of women in public ministry is as old as the gospel. Historian Richard Riss pays tribute to women whose amazing ministries have transformed lives throughout church history.[1]

WOMEN MARTYRS FOR THEIR FAITH

A kingdom woman will die defending her faith.

As Christianity spread, women along with their male contemporaries, lived their faith "even unto death," and through heroic deeds of love, helped build the foundations of God's Kingdom in their countries. In the early fourth century, Catherine of Alexandria defended the faith at Alexandria before philosophers and courtiers, before she was tortured to death by Maxentius, the son of the Roman Emperor, Maximian. At about the same time, Dorothy of Caesarea in Cappadocia was martyred (A.D. 313). As she was being led to her execution, Theophilus, a lawyer, taunted her, asking her for a basket of flowers and fruit. Soon afterward, a child came to her with a basket laden with roses and apples. She sent this to Theophilus, who as a result of this incident became a Christian and later gave his own life as a martyr.[2]

WOMEN FAITH CHAMPIONS

Macrina the Younger (A.D. 328–380) was founder of a religious community for women in the eastern church. With her brothers, Basil the Great and Gregory of Nyssa, she was a pioneer in the monastic life. She healed, prophesied, and actively spread the faith. John Chrysostom wrote of her that "she was a great organizer, and independent thinker, and as well educated as Basil himself." After the death of her mother, she reared and educated her younger brother Peter, who became Bishop of Sebaste.

Marcella (325–410) was an important teacher in the early church who was highly esteemed by Jerome. She was in the front lines in interacting with heretics and bringing them to a better understanding of Christian truth. Her palace on the Aventine Hill became a center of Christian influence. At one point, when a dispute arose in Rome concerning the meaning of the Scriptures, Jerome asked Marcella to settle it. Her Church of the Household was not only a house of study and prayer, but a center for deeds of Christian charity and sacrifice. It was here that another woman, Fabiola, received inspiration to establish the first hospitals in Rome. Marcella later established on the outskirts of Rome the first religious retreat for women.[3]

HISTORY OF WOMEN IN MINISTRY

It was also at Marcella's Church of the Household that Paula (347-404) and her daughter, Eustochium, first made their decision to assist Jerome in his Latin translation of the Bible. They went to Bethlehem in order to aid him in this work, revising and correcting his translations and making new Latin translations from the Hebrew and Greek texts. In turn, Jerome dedicated some of his books to them. Paula founded three convents and a monastery in Bethlehem, where Biblical manuscripts were copied. This became a model for what soon became the universal practice at monasteries for many centuries.

Genevieve (422–500) lived in Paris when Attila and his Huns invaded France in 451. She assured the inhabitants of Paris that God would protect them if they would pray. While the men prepared for battle, she persuaded the women to pray for hours in the church. Then, after Attila destroyed Orleans, he decided not to touch Paris. At a later time, she was said to have averted a famine in Paris and the surrounding cities by distributing miraculous gifts of bread.

Bridget, also known as Bride (455–523), inspired the convent system that made an indelible impact upon life in Ireland. After settling in Kildare, she built for herself and her female friends a house for refuge and devotion. As other houses were founded through her missionary efforts, she became known as the "mother abbess" of all of Ireland.

Theodora I (500–548), wife of the emperor Justinian, was an important and influential

Christian. A woman of outstanding intellect and learning, she was a moral reformer. Justinian, as Christian Emperor, was, for all practical purposes, head of the Church of his generation, and his wife, as Empress, shared his power to select church leaders. The inscription "Theodora Episcopa" or "Theodora, Bishop (fem.)" in a mosaic at the Basilica of Sts. Prudentia and Praexedis in Rome, may have been a reference to the Empress.

Hilda (614–680) was appointed by Aidan as abbess of the convent at Hartlepool in County Durham in 649. Ten years later, she founded a double monastery for men and women at Whitby in Yorkshire, which became world famous as a school of theology and literature. Five of her disciples became bishops and a sixth, Caedmon, became the earliest known English poet.

Hildegard of Bingen (1098–1179) was a German abbess, and writer known throughout all of Europe. Skilled in subjects as diverse as theology, medicine and politics, she did not hesitate to rebuke the sins of the greatest men of her time in both Church and state. She exerted a wide influence among many people, including the Emperor Frederick Barbarossa and various kings, prelates, and saints. Many miracles were attributed to her during her lifetime.

Clare (1193–1253) was co-founder, with Francis of Assisi, of the Poor Clares, a mendicant order which spread rapidly through Italy and into France, Germany, and Spain. In 1249, when she was lame, her convent was attacked by a group of Saracens. She told the sisters to carry her to the door of the monastery, then addressed the Saracens and prayed aloud that God would "deliver the defenseless children whom I have nourished with Thy love." She heard a voice answer "I will always have them in my keeping," and turning to the sisters, she said, "Fear not." At this moment, the Saracens scrambled down the walls of the cloister, recoiling from her valiant words. Clare's care for the poor was a tremendous inspiration to Elizabeth of Hungary (1207–1231), a princess who, in the last years of her short life, led a life of rigorous self-sacrifice and service to the poor and sick.

Some other significant women of the thirteenth through fifteenth centuries included Mechthild of Magdeburg, Gertrude the Great, Angela of Foligno, Bridget of Sweden, Catherine of Siena, Catherine of Sweden, Margery Kempe, Julian of Norwich, Joan of Arc, Catherine of Genoa, Isabella of Castile, and Margaret Beaufort.[4]

WOMEN ARE REFORMERS

During the Reformation, a member of the Bavarian nobility, Argula von Grumbach (1492–1563), challenged the Rector and all of the faculty of the University of Ingolstadt to a debate in which she would defend the principles of the Protestant Reformation. She offered to base this debate upon a translation of the Bible published prior to the outbreak of the Reformation. She was permitted to present her position in 1523 in Nuremberg before the heads of the Empire. Martin Luther wrote of her, "that most noble woman, Argula von Stauff, is there making a valiant fight with great spirit, boldness of speech and knowledge of Christ." Her extensive education and fine critical abilities enabled her to become a force to be reckoned with. She conducted church meetings in her home and officiated at funerals.

Two other important leaders of the Protestant Reformation were Margaret of Navarre (1492–1549) and her daughter, Jeanne d'Albret (1528-1572), the grandmother and mother of King Henry IV of France, who issued the Edict of Nantes, granting religious toleration to the French Protestants for almost a century. Jeanne d'Albret held services of the new Reformed faith in her palace apartment. A friend of John Calvin, she also used her palace as an institute for Reformation study.[5]

WOMEN LEADERS IN DENOMINATIONAL MOVEMENTS

During the Puritan era, Anne Hutchinson (1591–1643), became influential in Boston, and opened her home to large classes of women. It is estimated that as many as eighty overflowed to the doorsteps of her house, at a time when Boston had a population of roughly 1,000 people. These meetings grew rapidly, and soon men, also, began to attend. Among her loyal followers was Henry Vane, who served for a short time as governor of the Massachusetts Bay Colony. Within two years of her arrival from England, she had the strongest following of any leader in the entire colony. Her large following, coupled with her strong exegetical and homiletical skills, deep Christian commitment and insightful understanding of spiritual truths, may have incurred the jealousy of several New England ministers, who became uncomfortable enough with her successes that she was accused of heresy and banished from the Massachusetts Bay Colony in 1638.

Margaret Fell (1614–1702), the mother of Quakerism, was an English peeress and wife of Judge Thomas Fell, member of the Long Parliament and Vice-Chancellor of Lancaster. Her home became a place of refuge and renewal for the persecuted Quakers for almost fifty years. She was arrested for holding Quaker meetings in her home, Swarthmoor Hall, and imprisoned for four years. After her release from prison, she visited Quakers in jails and traveled on horseback with her daughters and servants to remote farms and villages as an itinerant preacher. Many people sought wisdom and advice from her, including Thomas Salthouse, and, of course, George Fox, who married her a number of years after the death of her husband. Because she had his blessing in her preaching ministry, she wrote many tracts and letters on the subject of women in ministry.

Madame Guyon (1648–1717) was a French woman who was imprisoned on several occasions for long periods of time because of her beliefs, but she was never known to complain about this. An author of forty books, including a twenty-volume commentary of the Bible, she had a wide following, particularly in France and Switzerland. Among those profoundly influenced by her ministry was Archbishop Francois Fenelon.

The founder of the first Methodist congregation in America was Barbara Heck (1734–1804).

In England, Lady Selina Hastings, Countess of Huntingdon (1707–1791), founder of the Calvinistic Methodist denomination during the Evangelical Awakening, functioned as a bishop by virtue of her right as a peeress to appoint Anglican clergymen as household chaplains and assign their duties, and to purchase presentation rights to chapels, enabling her to decide who would conduct services and preach. Among the many chaplains whom she appointed and continued to finance for many decades was George Whitefield. In 1779, after sixty chapels were already functioning under her auspices, this practice was disallowed by a consistory court of London. Therefore, in order to continue to function, she was able, under the Toleration Act, to register her chapels as dissenting places of worship, known as "The Countess of Huntingdon's Connexion."

Lady Selina frequently invited members of the aristocracy to her home to hear the preaching of the Wesleys, Whitefield, Isaac Watts, Philip Doddridge, Benjamin Ingham, John Fletcher, John Berridge, William Romaine, Henry Venn, and others. She founded Trevecca House on property adjoining the home of Howel Harris. A seminary for the training of ministers for all denominations, its first president was John Fletcher. Joseph Benson eventually became headmaster on John Wesley's recommendation. George Whitefield preached the inaugural sermon when it opened in 1768.[6]

WOMEN PREACHERS IN AMERICAN HISTORY

In America, two important preachers during the first years of the Second Awakening (1800–1808) were Deborah Pierce of Paris, N.Y. and Martha Howell of Utica. Phoebe Palmer (1807–1874), "The Mother of the Holiness Movement" began her ministry in 1835 with her Tuesday Meetings for the Promotion of Holiness, which continued for 39 years in New York City, where she lived with her husband, who was a physician. Hundreds of Methodist preachers, including at least five bishops, were profoundly affected by her ministry. The success of Phoebe Palmer's informal meetings encouraged other women to conduct the same type of ministry, and dozens of them sprang up throughout North America. These meetings brought together Christians of many denominations under the leadership of women, particularly among Methodists, Congregationalists, Episcopalians, Baptists, and Quakers.

In 1858, Walter Palmer, Phoebe's husband, purchased the periodical GUIDE TO HOLINESS, which under her able editorship, grew in circulation from 13,000 to 30,000 subscribers. She traveled widely with her husband, conducting evangelistic meetings during the summer months. In the fall of 1857, she and her husband traveled to Hamilton, Ontario, where they attracted crowds of several thousand people when an afternoon prayer meeting became a ten-day revival meeting during which four hundred people were converted to Christ. They experienced similar successes in New York City and in England, where they preached for four years to packed houses at Leeds, Sheffield, Manchester, Birmingham, and dozens of other places. It is estimated that within her lifetime, Phoebe Palmer brought over 25,000 people to faith in Christ.

Catherine Booth (1829–1890), with her husband, William Booth, founded the Christian Revival Association in 1865 and the Salvation Army in 1878. The Booths regarded the active participation of women to be vital to Christianity. Before 1865, when they were still Methodists, Catherine began preaching. Soon after her pulpit debut, her husband became ill, and his slow recovery paved the way for her own preaching ministry. For a time, he was so ill that she had to take over his entire preaching circuit. She eventually became one of the most famous female preachers of England, and her last sermon was delivered to an audience of 50,000 people.

Hannah Whitall Smith, author of THE CHRISTIAN'S SECRET OF A HAPPY LIFE (1875) catalyzed the development of the Holiness movement in Britain and throughout Europe. Her activities in England led to the Keswick Convention in 1874.[7]

PENTECOSTAL WOMEN IN HISTORY

Carrie Judd Montgomery was a healing evangelist of considerable prominence beginning in 1879, and became a founding member, along with A. B. Simpson, of the Christian and Missionary Alliance in 1887. She later became a part of the Pentecostal revival and was ordained a minister by the Assemblies of God in 1917, continuing in ministry until 1946.

Maria B. Woodworth-Etter was also involved in the Holiness movement before she rose to prominence as an early Pentecostal leader. In 1884, she was licensed to preach by the Churches of God general conference, founded by John Winebrenner in 1825. Within a few months of this time her meetings were already beginning to receive national press coverage, and in the late 1880s she started twelve churches, added 1,000 members, erected six church buildings, and started several Sunday Schools. Her work at this time resulted in the licensing of twelve preachers. The revivals that she held at this time were accompanied with unusual manifestations of God's power, many healings, and mass conversions. During the early Pentecostal movement, Woodworth-Etter was in continual demand, becoming a featured speaker at the Worldwide Pentecostal Camp Meeting at Arroyo Seco, California, in April 1913. She founded the Woodworth-Etter Tabernacle in western Indianapolis in 1918, which she pastored until her death in 1924.

Beginning in 1906 and 1907, Florence L. Crawford, Mabel Smith, Ivey Campbell, and Rachel A. Sizelove were some of the first women to spread the blessings of the early Pentecostal revival through their separate itinerant ministries. Florence Crawford planted and pastored several churches in the Pacific Northwest, founding and becoming general overseer of the Apostolic Faith Church based in Portland, Oregon, which later became part of the Open Bible Standard Denomination.

Other pioneers of the Pentecostal movement in the U.S. included Mrs. Scott Ladd, who opened a Pentecostal mission in Des Moines in 1907, the Duncan sisters, who opened the Rochester Bible Training School at Elim Faith Home, "Mother" Barnes of St. Louis, Missouri, who, with her son-in-law, B. F. Lawrence, held tent meetings in southern Illinois in the spring of 1908, and Marie Burgess, who preached in Chicago, Toledo, Detroit, and New York City, where she founded Glad Tidings

Hall, which soon became an important center for the spread of the Pentecostal revival. Another early Pentecostal pioneer in New York was Miss Maud Williams (Haycroft).[8]

Pentecostal Women Preachers in Canadian and European History

In Canada, some early pioneers of the Pentecostal movement included Ellen Hebden in Toronto, Ella M.Goff in Winnipeg, Alice B. Garrigus in Newfoundland, the Davis sisters in the Maritime provinces, Mrs. C. E. Baker in Montreal, and Zelma Argue throughout all of the Canadian provinces. Aimee Semple McPherson of Ingersoll, Ontario, began a preaching ministry in 1915 which began in Toronto and took her along the U.S. Eastern Seaboard, and across the United States in 1918. She eventually founded Angelus Temple in 1923, where she continued as senior pastor until her death in 1944.

An outstanding authoress and minister at the turn of the century was Jesse Penn-Lewis who was directly involved with the revival in Wales. Evan Roberts, the chief evangelist of the Welsh revival joined Mrs. Lewis in penning some of her writings on the overcoming life. Mrs. Lewis had a wide public ministry. Perhaps the most popular book she wrote was WAR ON THE SAINTS, a book on spiritual warfare.[9]

A Woman with an Exceptional Healing and Miracle Ministry

Kathryn Kuhlman's ministry began in the summer of 1923. After her ordination by the Evangelical Church Alliance in Joliet, Illinois, she established the Denver Revival Tabernacle in 1935, which she pastored for three years. In the mid-1940s, she went to Franklin, Pennsylvania, where she began to thrive as a preacher and radio evangelist. Many people were healed with notable miracles at her meetings beginning in 1947, and she gained a reputation as one of the world's outstanding healing evangelists, carrying on as a leading figure during the charismatic movement until her death in 1976.[10]

Charismatic Women Pastors

A few of the women working as Pentecostal pastors during the charismatic movement of the 1960s and 1970s included Charlotte Baker, Myrtle D. Beall, Helen Beard, Aimee Cortese, Sue Curran, B. Maureen Gaglardi, Anne Giminez, Ione Glaeser, Hattie Hammond, Alpha A. Henson, Marilyn Hickey, Violet Kitely, Janet Kreis, Freda Lindsay, Fuchsia T. Pickett, Iverna Tompkins, and Rachel Titus. A sampling of a few of the other women who were vital during the time of the charismatic movement as speakers, authors, or evangelists, would include Eleanor and Roberta Armstrong, Rita Bennett, Edith Blumhofer, Hazel Bonawitz, Roxanne Brant, Mary Ann Brown, Shirley Carpenter, Jean Darnall, Josephine Massynberde Ford, Katie Fortune, Shirlee Green, Nina Harris,

> Sue Malachuk, Daisy Osborn, Dorothy Ranaghan, Agnes Sanford, Gwen Shaw, Bernice Smith, Ruth Carter Stapleton, Jean Stone, Joni Eareckson Tada, and Corrie Ten Boom. Mother Teresa was also an outstanding woman who ministered in the helps ministry to the poor of India.
>
> The women mentioned here are, of course, a mere sampling of important figures who have been mightily used of God in every conceivable capacity of leadership in the church throughout history.[11]

The biblical examples above highlight how God has historically used women to have His will done in the Earth, and there are many more examples of how God has used women to fulfill His mandate than I have room to describe here. God has been using women effectively in ministry all throughout history in a way that builds the kingdom up instead of tearing it down, as some fear will happen by allowing women in the pulpit.

Kingdom woman, it's time for you to join these women by stepping into your calling. Throw off the chains that have been holding you back from your ministry, walk forward in holiness and obedience, and watch to see how God will use you and His anointing on your life to effect change in your family, community, nation, and the world.

Epilogue

A PROPHETIC WORD TO THE KINGDOM WOMAN: ARISE AND SHINE!

> *Arise, shine; for thy light is come, and the glory of the Lord is risen upon thee. For, behold, the darkness shall cover the earth, and gross darkness the people: but the Lord shall arise upon thee, and his glory shall be seen upon thee.*
> —Isaiah 60:1–2

For the Lord says:

These are the days that I call forth kingdom women to arise and shine. Yes, your light has come, and My glory has risen upon you. Surely, My glory shall be seen upon you. For these are the days that I call you forth for such a time as this. Who shall I send? Who shall go? Who shall answer the call to be that kingdom woman I have created them to be?

Know that the kingdom is inside of you.

For these are the days that I am raising up the modern-day Deborahs. They shall stand *as judges in government and in the political arena. Women mayors, women senators, and women presidents are arising.*

For these are the days I am raising up the modern-day Esthers with great courage to deliver their people.

I'm raising up the modern-day Ruths who understand.

I am raising up the modern-day Annas, who will pray, "Your kingdom come; Your will be done."

I am raising up the modern-day Junias and Priscillas.

Kingdom women are rising up as a mighty army. They will collaborate with men to deliver My counsel in My kingdom, for in Me there is neither male or female.

I am calling women of color to a greater level of power, glory, and influence. No longer shall they draw back in fear, but they will walk in faith, power, and glory. They will activate, teach, and train other women. Yes, women who have a covenant with Me, I shall crown them with My glory.

"He that is holy, he that is true, he that hath the key of David, he that opens, and no man shuts; and shuts, and no man opens" [Rev. 3:7]. God said, "I know your sacrifices, "and behold, I have set before thee an open door, and no man can shut it" [Rev. 3:7].

Think it not strange that I'm causing women to arise in the Earth like never before. Think it not strange I call women apostles, women prophets, women pastors, apostolic women to stand in positions of leadership in authority, for in the days to come women will stand in high places of government. Women presidents. I'm opening new doors where in time past doors were shut. But now I open doors that no man can shut for women to do what they could not do in time past. For these are days I'm shifting the mind-set of men and women. I'm releasing rivers of revelation concerning kingdom women, saith the Lord.

I have put keys of authority into your hands, that you may activate the mandate, the mantle, the ministry that I place inside of you, that you may walk in wisdom, understanding, counsel, might, knowledge, and the fear of the Lord—not the fear of man, for who is man that Thou art mindful of him?

Kingdom woman, I give you keys; I give you authority to lock and unlock, to access My kingdom through prayer and intercession, through decrees and declarations, and yes, through your obedience. I give to you the scepter of righteousness to rule and reign from a place of holiness in the heavens and in the Earth, saith the Lord.

Apostolic Woman Arise

Kingdom woman, "Arise, shine, for your light has come, and the glory of the Lord has risen upon you" (Isa. 60:1, ESV).

Kingdom woman, you are called for such a time as

this. Proclaim a *kairos* time, a clarion call. There are women all around the world from different walks of life who may sense the call of God on their life. They are hidden treasures in the earth. They are secretly crying out in their hearts for a Macedonian call for women in ministry, saying, "Come over into Macedonia, and help us" (Acts 16:9). After all, no one becomes successful by themselves. When we support each other we all win. Kingdom woman, you have been given a charge not only for your life but for other women, to prophetically discern the call of God on the lives of others and help them fulfill their destiny as Naomi did with Ruth. In Genesis 1:27–28, God is calling you to legislate in the earth.

It is a challenge to occupy territory where no one may have gone before, but kingdom women are challenged to walk on water, to walk on uncharted territory—especially when we live in a world where not everyone accepts women in ministry leadership. But the earth is groaning for the manifestation of the sons of God.

Kingdom woman, God is calling you to be a trendsetter, a trailblazer, a pioneer; to compel other women by releasing uncompressed, undiluted prophetic decrees into the atmosphere.

Kingdom women and apostolic women are arising. "And it shall come to pass...that I will pour out my spirit upon all flesh; and your sons and daughters shall prophesy" (Joel 2:28). Kingdom women are coming from behind the walls of the church to reach and teach other women of all colors, cultures and countries—black, white, Hispanic, Asian, African and European. God is raising up apostolic, spiritual midwives to give birth to purpose and destiny, connecting with women around the world for global glory gatherings for the next generation.

God is saying, "Who shall I send? Who shall go? Who shall answer the call?" Kingdom woman, arise and say, "Here I am. Send me. I shall go." Apostolic woman, arise.

Appendix

WOMANOLOGY

WOMANOLOGY IS THE study of female behavior, ways, and intelligence. By nature, women are nurturers of life. Godly women demonstrate humility, love, and compassion. They also desire to be spiritual nurturers who help advance the kingdom.

Because of their influence, power, and authority, women in leadership roles in the church are often accused of being a Jezebel, when this is often not the case. Women should not allow this stigma and accusation to prevent them from pursuing their God-given calling or from serving others and leading with passion. In those moments of opposition, a kingdom woman's tenacity, steadfast faith, and strength emerge—and lives around her are changed.

The following twelve women in the Bible are powerful examples from history of the impact kingdom women have on their circle of influence and beyond. Their decision to trust the Lord and surrender their lives to His leading, is transforming and inspiring the faith walk of believers, even generations after their passing. Like ripples in a pool, the results of their faith in action have echoed through generations. That is the legacy of a kingdom woman.

1. Abigail: In Hebrew, the name *Abigail* means "joy of the father, "father rejoiced," or "the father's joy."[1] The Old Testament tells us Abigail was wise and beautiful (1 Sam. 25:3). Her discretion and unmatched beauty caught David's eye, and after her husband Nabal died, she became King David's third wife.

2. Anna: The name *Anna* is Latin, though it has its roots in the Greek name Avva and the Hebrew name Hannah. It means "favor," "grace," or "beautiful."[2] Luke 2:36–37 tells us that Anna was a prophetess. We are not all called to be prophets, but as kingdom women we have favor and grace upon our lives as spiritual Annas on the Earth.

3. Bathsheba: Bathsheba was the wife of Uriah and, afterward, of David, with whom she became the mother of Solomon. (See 2 Samuel 11, 12.) *Easton's Bible Dictionary* notes that "Bathsheba took a prominent part in securing the succession of Solomon to the throne (1 Kings 1:11, 16–21)."[3] Her name means "the daughter of an oath."[4] She stands in history as a reminder that when we make a solemn vow to God, as kingdom women it's important to keep that promise.

4. Deborah: Deborah was a prophetess and the only female judge of Israel. (Judges 4–5).

5. Esther: Esther, who was also known as Hadassah, was a beautiful, young Jewish woman who was chosen by the King Ahasuerus of Persia to be his queen. She came to the rescue of her people when, after fasting for three days, she went into the king's palace to petition for their lives after an evil decree to destroy the Jews had been passed.

6. Hannah: Hannah's womb was closed in a time in history in which it was both personally painful and a public shame to be barren. She cried out to the Lord at the temple, telling God that if He gave her a son, she would give him up to become a priest (1 Sam. 1:20). God granted her request, and her son became the prophet Samuel, who God used to anoint David king.

7. Junia: Junia was highly regarded by the apostle Paul. Different versions of Romans 16:7 indicate that Paul either referred to Junia as an apostle herself or explained that she was well thought of by the apostles.[5]

8. Lydia: Lydia of Thyatira was a businesswoman and a deaconess. In Acts 16:12–15 we read that she was Paul's first convert in

Philippi, making her also his first convert to Christianity in Europe. When she was saved, she went and gathered family and friends so that they too could know the truth that would set them free. Later, after Paul and Silas were released from prison, she took them into her home to care for them. Some historians believe that since Lydia's home "became a center of Christian fellowship in Philippi," it's possible that the first Christian church was birthed in her house.[6] The Scriptures describe this faithful woman as a worshiper of God and a God fearer.

9. Mary: There are two Marys of note in the Scriptures. The first is the Virgin Mary, the mother of Jesus. The second was the sister of Lazarus and Martha. (See Luke 10:38; John 11:1–2.)

10. Priscilla: Priscilla, who ministered along with her husband Aquila, was an influential leader in the early church. Apostle Paul described the couple as his "helpers" in Christ Jesus (Rom. 16:3). Some historians have suggested that Priscilla might have been a deaconess.[7]

11. Ruth: Ruth was a Moabite woman who accompanied her Israelite mother-in-law, Naomi, back to Bethlehem after their husbands passed away. She is revered for her faithfulness to Naomi and decision to trust the God of Israel, which is expressed

poignantly in Ruth 1:16, in which Ruth tells her mother-in-law, "Wherever you go, I will go; And wherever you lodge, I will lodge; Your people shall be my people, And your God, my God" (NKJV). She is also revered for her humility and the way she honored Naomi and Boaz, the kinsman-redeemer who took Ruth to be his wife (Ruth 4:13).

12. Sarah: Sarah was Abraham's wife and his half-sister. Like Hannah, she was childless, though Sarah endured many years of waiting between God's promise to make her a mother and the birth of her son, Isaac. (See Genesis 17.)

NOTES

CHAPTER 1—WHO IS THE KINGDOM WOMAN?

1. Finis J. Dake, *Dake Annotated Reference Bible, King James Version* (Lawrenceville, GA: Dake Publishing. 2002), s.v. "1 Corinthians 14:34."
2. Strong's Concordance, available at BibleHub, s.v. "Entos," accessed February 15, 2018, https://biblehub.com/greek/1787.htm
3. Merriam-Webster.com, s.v. "kingdom," https://www.merriam-webster.com/dictionary/kingdom.
4. Ibid.
5. *Strong's Concordance*, available at BibleHub, s.v. "Basileia," accessed February 28, 2018, https://biblehub.com/greek/932.htm.

CHAPTER 2—THE CHARACTER OF THE KINGDOM WOMAN

1. Ann S. Spangler and Jean E. Syswerda, *Women of the Bible* (Grand Rapids, MI: Zondervan, 2007), 115.
2. Betty Miller, "What the Bible Says About Women in Ministry," *BibleResources.org*, accessed March 2, 2018, at https://bibleresources.org/women-in-ministry.
3. Matthew Henry, *Matthew Henry's Commentary on the Bible* (Grand Rapids, MI: Christian Classics Ethereal Library, n.d.).
4. Matthew Henry, *An Exposition of the Old and New Testament: Wherein Each Chapter is Summed Up in Its Contents: Joshua-Esther. 1839* (N.p.: J. Robinson, 1839).
5. Dictionary.com, s.v. "diamond," accessed March 2, 2018, http://www.dictionary.com/browse/diamond.
6. Dake, *Dake Annotated Reference Bible, King James Version*, 1108.

CHAPTER 3—THE KINGDOM WOMAN ON A MISSION

1. Merriam-Webster.com, s.v. "mandate," https://www.merriamwebster.com/dictionary/mandate.
2. *Oxford American Writer's Thesaurus*, 3rd edition (Oxford: Oxford University Press, 2012), s.v. "mandate," accessed March 2, 2018, at Google Books.
3. *Oxford English Living Dictionaries Online*, s.v. "mandate," accessed February 19, 2018, https://en.oxforddictionaries.com/definition/mandate.

4. Dictionary.com, s.v. "mandate," http://www.dictionary.com/browse/mandate.
5. Merriam-Webster.com, s.v. "dream," https://www.merriam-webster.com/dictionary/dream.

Chapter 4—The Kingdom Woman—Tested and Proven, Delivered and Set Free

1. *Oxford English Living Dictionaries Online*, s.v. "resilience," https://en.oxforddictionaries.com/definition/resilience.

Chapter 5—Anointed and Called

1. Frederick Aldolphus Packard, *The Union Bible Dictionary* (Philadelphia, PA: American Sunday School Union, 1839), 409.
2. *Oxford English Living Dictionaries Online*, s.v. "mantle," accessed February 19, 2018, https://en.oxforddictionaries.com/definition/mantle.

Chapter 6—Carrier of the Glory

1. *Webster's 1828 American Dictionary of the English Language—Online Edition*, s.v. "holiness," accessed February 21, 2018, http://webstersdictionary1828.com/Holiness.

Chapter 7—Authority, Power, and Demonstration

1. Merriam-Webster.com, s.v. "legislate," accessed February 27, 2018, https://www.merriam-webster.com/dictionary/legislate.

Chapter 8—What Does the Bible Say About Women in Ministry and Leadership?

1. Miller, "What the Bible Says About Women in Ministry," BibleResources.org.
2. Ibid.
3. Dake, *Dake Annotated Reference Bible, King James Version*, s.v."1 Corinthians 14:34."
4. *Strong's Concordance*, available at BibleHub, s.v. "Abigail," accessed February 28, 2018, http://biblehub.com/hebrew/26.htm.
5. Dake, *Dake Annotated Reference Bible, King James Version*, s.v, "1 Samuel 25."

6. Frank E. Gaebelein, *The Expositor's Bible Commentary, Abridged Edition* (Grand Rapids, MI: Zondervan, 2004).
7. Eugene E. Carpenter, *Asbury Bible Commentary*, ed. Wayne McCown (Grand Rapids, MI: Zondervan, 1992), s.v. "Philippians 4:2–3."
8. Matthew Henry, *Matthew Henry's Commentary on the Bible*.

Chapter 11—The Kingdom Woman Serving in Fivefold Ministry

1. Hakeem Collins, *Born to Prophesy* (Lake Mary, FL: Creation House, 2013), 122.
2. Miller, "What the Bible Says About Women in Ministry," BibleResources.org.
3. Matthew Henry, *Matthew Henry's Commentary on the Bible*, 132–133.
4. Collins, *Born to Prophesy*, 123–124.
5. Dean Snyder, "Apostles, Prophets, Evangelists, Pastors, Teachers: Understanding the Five Core Leadership Functions in Ephesians 4," Foundry United Methodist Church, accessed March 3, 2018, at http://www.foundryumc.org/apostles-prophets-evangelists-pastors-teachers-understanding-five-core-leadership-functions-ephesian.
6. *Strong's Concordance*, available at BibleHub.com, s.v. "poimén," accessed March 1, 2018, http://biblehub.com/greek/4166.htm.
7. "Ephesians 4:11 Ministry Teams and the Apostolic Movement," *5-Fold Global Ministries*, accessed March 1, 2018, http://www.5foldglobal.org/files/resources-leaders.e411.pdf.
8. Toh Nee Lim, "As Ye Preach, Saying, The Kingdom of Heaven Is at Hand," Evangel.org, http://evangel.org.ph/as-as-ye-preach-saying-the-kingdom-of-heaven-is-at-hand/.
9. "Ephesians 4:11 Ministry Teams and the Apostolic Movement," *5-Fold Global Ministries*.

Chapter 12—The Kingdom Woman: A Legacy of Influence

1. Miller, "What the Bible Says About Women in Ministry," BibleResources.org.

2. Richard Riss, "Women Throughout History Served as Leaders," accessed at Betty Miller, "Women in Ministry: What the Bible Says," BibleResources.org.
3. Ibid.
4. Ibid.
5. Ibid.
6. Ibid.
7. Ibid.
8. Ibid.
9. Ibid.
10. Ibid.
11. Ibid.

Appendix A—Womanology

1. *Baby Center*, s.v. "Abigail," accessed June 17, 2018, https://www.babycenter.com/baby-names-abigail-15.htm.
2. 2. *Wikipedia*, s.v. "Anna," accessed June 10, 2018, https://en.wikipedia.org/wiki/Anna_(given_name).
3. *Easton's Bible Dictionary*, s.v. "Bathsheba," available at *BibleHub*, accessed June 17, 2018, http://biblehub.com/topical/b/bathsheba.htm.
4. *International Standard Bible Encyclopedia*, s.v. "Bathsheba," available at *BibleHub*, accessed June 17, 2018, http://biblehub.com/topical/b/bathsheba.htm.
5. Dennis J. Preato, "Junia, a Female Apostle," *God's Word to Women*, available at *BibleHub*, accessed June 10, 2018, https://godswordtowomen.org/juniapreato.htm.
6. *BibleGateway*, s.v. "Lydia," accessed June 10, 2018, https://www.biblegateway.com/resources/all-women-bible/Lydia.
7. *Wikipedia*, s.v. "Priscilla and Aquila," accessed June 10, 2018, https://en.wikipedia.org/wiki/Priscilla_and_Aquila.

www.ingramcontent.com/pod-product-compliance
Lightning Source LLC
Chambersburg PA
CBHW052023070526
44584CB00016B/1876